Jack Imel:
My Years with Lawrence Welk
As a Tap-Dancing Marimba Player

All rights reserved. No part of this book may be reproduced or transmitted in any form or by any means, electronic or mechanical, including photocopying, recording, or by an information storage and retrieval system without written permission from the author, except for the inclusion of brief quotations in a review.

Copyright @ 2013 Jack Imel
All rights reserved.
ISBN: 1492258709
ISBN-13: 978-1492258704

Library of Congress Number: 2013917734

Cover Design by Richard Whetstone
Interior by Linda Rae Roggensack

CreateSpace Independent Publishing Platform
North Charleston, South Carolina

JACK IMEL:

My Years with Lawrence Welk as a Tap-Dancing Marimba Player

By Jack Imel

CONTENTS

In Memory vii
Dedication ix
Acknowledgements xi
My Indiana Home 13
Basketball Dreams: Plan B 23
Jack's Got Talent! 29
Anchors Aweigh 35
Chance of a Lifetime 39
You're Hired! 47
The Welk Family 55
The Imel Family 59
All I Want for Christmas 63
Welk's Bad Boy 69
The Sixties 75
Bomb Threats and Buffalo Herds 85
The Show Goes Live 91
Turn off the Bubble Machine 95
The Seventies 99
Summers on the Road 107
Seeing Stars 117
Adios, au Revoir, Aufwiedersehn 121
Over the Ocean Blue 127
Keep a Song in Your Heart 133
Bound for Branson 135
One-Nighters 141
Meanwhile, Back Home in Indiana 145
The Family Tree 151
The Golden Years 163
Oh Yes, I'd Like to Do It Again 169

IN MEMORY

This book is written in memory of my son Terrence (Terry) Mark who died of a major heart attack at the age of 38. He had a wonderful outlook on life with a great sense of humor. Norma and I miss him more than words can say, but we know now that he is in the Kingdom of God. He left behind a son, Forrest, and Terry would be so proud of him. Terry remains in the hearts of all who knew him.

Our youngest son, Terry, died not long after this photo was taken.

THIS BOOK IS DEDICATED TO MY FAMILY

A gala evening to celebrate our fiftieth wedding anniversary was a gift from our children, a night we will always cherish. Norma and I feel blessed to have such a wonderful family, (from left) Tim Imel, Cindy Imel Buttner, Norma Imel, Jack Imel, Debbie Imel Charton, and Greg Imel.

ACKNOWLEDGEMENTS

This book represents seventy years worth of stories from my life in show business. I'm grateful to friends and family who encouraged me to put it down in writing. None of this would have been possible without my parents' belief, when I was just a boy, that I had talent. I also appreciate Lawrence Welk for taking a chance on a young tap-dancing, marimba-playing sailor.

I'd like to express my gratitude to Linda Rae Roggensack for the countless hours she spent editing, organizing, and formatting my stories to create this book. I also appreciate the help of Sally Parry and my son Timothy Imel for transcribing my recorded notes. In addition, I want to thank my longtime friend Max Donaldson for his suggestions and assistance in putting this together. Richard Whetstone designed the cover and did a fine job of preparing all the photographs, many of which were dog-eared and faded, culled from my scrapbooks. And finally, a special thanks to Claire Graca for batting cleanup and design consulting.

My heart is filled with gratitude for all the friendships I formed working with the Welk Musical Family mentioned in this book. In particular, I appreciate the support from Mary Lou Metzger, Ava Barber, and the Lennon Sisters in the final process of writing these stories. I'm also indebted to all the loyal fans that watched our show, and to this day, continue to keep us alive on PBS.

Most of all, I want to thank my children and my beautiful wife, Norma, for standing by me with love, encouragement, and patience.

One

MY INDIANA HOME

I'm a tap dancer and a marimba player—both at the same time. Now this may not thrill the hearts of too many people, but I've been able to make a living at it since I was twelve years old. I spent twenty-five wonderful years as a performer with *The Lawrence Welk Show*, seventeen of those years as associate producer of the television show, and I produced all of his road shows. For whatever reason, everyone on the show called me Ace. I have a wonderful wife and great parents, and being born and raised in Portland, Indiana, certainly had its advantages.

Portland had a great county fair, good basketball teams, and was the birthplace of the girl I married. That's right, I married my hometown sweetheart. Her maiden name was Norma Jean Denney, and we've been together since junior high school. She is without a doubt the best thing that ever happened to me. We have been married for over sixty years, and I love her more now than I did on our wedding day. Any success or accomplishments that I may have achieved would not have happened without Norma. She not only supported my career choice, but put up with all of my nonsense. We were blessed with five children, and she has been a wonderful mother. I could write a book just about her.

I was fortunate to have a mother and father, Jennings and Opel Imel, who not only loved me, but dedicated themselves to my well-being. I was an only child, and they did all they could to encourage what talent I had so it didn't go to waste. People have asked me which came first, the dancing or the marimba? Well, it was the dancing. Thanks to my mother, I started taking dance lessons at the age of four. My teacher's name was Maureen Lucas, and I can still remember a routine she taught me. I tap danced on top of a wooden drum, dressed up like Uncle Sam, to the song "Stars and Stripes Forever." The first time I ever performed this routine in front of an audience was for my mother's sorority at the Portland Country Club when I was five years old.

Marjorie Jean Fields, my dancing teacher, predicted a bright future for me in show business.

My second teacher was Marjorie Jean Fields who ran a dance school in Muncie, about thirty miles away. My mother drove me there every week for lessons for almost twelve years. Marjorie Jean was a great teacher, and you just don't find someone of her caliber in a smaller town. She later moved to Hollywood and became an assistant to Nick Castle, who was one of the top choreographers in motion pictures.

There were occasions, however, when Marjorie Jean could be hard as nails, especially if I didn't practice or apply myself. And that was my problem. I hated to practice. I must say, you won't make it in the entertainment business unless you practice, work hard, and dedicate yourself. I can remember sitting in the back seat of our car on the way to take my lessons, trying to remember what Marjorie Jean had taught me the week before.

She sent me home crying more than once, but it was my fault, not hers. Mom constantly had to remind me to go out on the back porch and practice.

Dance schools used to have what they called dance reviews where the parents, relatives, and friends show up to see if you have improved from the year before. So when a review was a few weeks away, my practice habits suddenly took priority, and all I thought about were my routines. I didn't want to make a fool of myself, especially in front of my parents. One thing about Marjorie Jean, if you did your routines well and had a lot of personality, she made you feel like a star. Thank God and eventual hard work, my routines always came out okay.

I think my mother could have done something in show business herself because she had an instinct for knowing what was good and what was bad, and she knew what people liked. I sort of doubt that being an entertainer ever entered her mind, although she did play a little piano by ear, and I thought she was quite good. Her father was a doctor and taught medicine at Indiana University-Fort Wayne. He also served as mayor of Portland and ran for the U.S. Congress in 1920.

Now, about my father: He was a quiet sort of person who always had a smile on his face. In fact, his nickname was Happy. Being one of eight brothers with two sisters, he didn't get the attention that he later gave to me when I was growing up. He had to quit school after the eighth grade and got a job as a meat cutter to help support his family. During the First World War, he was a mess sergeant, and after the war, he came home and married my mother. He and his brother Jack, my namesake, started their own business in Portland, a meat market called Imel Brothers Grocery Store. They did well, and the store lasted over thirty years.

My parents owned a home on the west side of Portland and had a farm about five miles out of town. Dad paid for all those dance lessons of mine—I couldn't do anything wrong in my father's eyes. I remember one time my mother told him to give me a spanking for something I had done. He took me into the bathroom, shut the door and said, "Okay, Jack, now I'll hit my leg and then you yell out. But if you ever do that again, you'll get a real spanking." My dad worked hard all his life, and I would like to think some of it rubbed off on me. My parents are both gone now, and I sure miss them, but I guess that's part of life.

Talent shows have always been a means of discovery for someone trying to make a career out of show business. Radio station WOWO in Fort Wayne used to hold a talent show for young people every week. When I was nine years old, Mom asked me if I would like to try out. "Sure, why not," I said.

Marjorie Jean had taught me a couple of showy routines, and it sounded like a good idea. So my parents drove me to Fort Wayne, and I experienced my first audition. I can remember being really nervous, but I did my routine and tried to give it as much personality and showmanship as I could. When I finished, the man in charge told my mother that I was okay, but tap dancing didn't work for radio. People had to be able to see it. I was disappointed, but on the way home Mom told me there would be other chances.

We were almost home when my mother turned to me and said, "What you need to do is combine some music with your dancing. You should learn to play a musical instrument, something you could play standing up. But instead of just standing, you could tap dance while you play it." She thought for a moment and then said, "I've got it, a xylophone."

Remember, I was only nine years old and didn't have the slightest idea what she was talking about, but you can bet I was going to find out. A few weeks later I came home from school, walked in the house, and there in the living room was a xylophone. To me it looked like something from outer space.

As I mentioned, my mother played piano, and she knew the chords to a song called "Bye Bye Blues." She took pieces of tape and placed them on some of the keys of my new instrument. Now, if I hit the keys with tape on them in the right order, I could play "Bye Bye Blues." The lessons were about to begin. I would hit a note, and she would say "Dance." I hit another note, and she would say "Dance."

This went on for six months, and finally I could play "Bye Bye Blues" on the xylophone and tap dance at the same time. I had no idea what notes I was playing, but if I hit the taped keys in the right order, I was home free. She told the Moose Club in Portland what I could do, and they agreed to let me perform there. The Moose always held a dance on Saturday nights, and it looked like I was going to be the floor show. This was the moment of truth. Would the audience like it, or would I lay an egg? Well, I'm happy to say they not only liked it, they yelled

"More, more!" But how could I do more? It was the only song I knew, so I played it three times that night. Mom and Dad were very proud.

This was the start of a career that would last for more than seventy years, thanks to my parents. They knew that playing the xylophone meant taking music lessons—no more tape on the keys. Xylophone teachers were not that common where we lived, but Mom found out about Jack Kurkowski in Richmond, Indiana, who had a xylophone band and gave lessons. She contacted him, and I studied with him for almost four years. He taught me how to read music, and I learned a lot more songs.

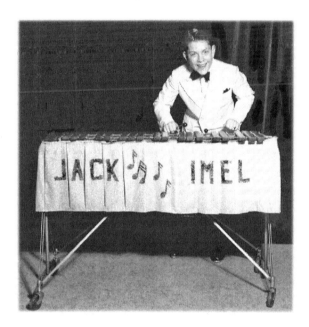

I was already a professional at twelve years old.

Now it may seem like my childhood was nothing but tap dancing and xylophones, but it wasn't. I really had a normal life growing up. I'll never forget my seventh birthday. My parents had a party for me, and I think every kid in Portland was there. A few of them are still living in Portland, and I make sure I see them every time I go back to visit. I love that town. The people are friendly and down to earth, and it was a great place to grow up. I still take the hometown paper just to keep up with what's going on. Later on, whenever Lawrence Welk introduced me on his television show, I always asked him beforehand to mention that my hometown was Portland, Indiana. He appreciated that because he came from an even smaller town called Strasburg, North Dakota.

When I was a kid, my father used to take me fishing during school vacations. At least twice a year we went with some of his brothers to Long Lake in northern Indiana, and I really looked forward to it. My mother always took me to a Chinese restaurant in Muncie after my dance lessons, and I have great memories of that too.

Another thing I really enjoyed was the Jay County Fair, which was held in Portland and considered one of the finest county fairs in the state. Since my dad owned a meat market, he opened a grocery store every year at the county fair. During Fair Week, I spent every day and night there. Next to Christmas, that was my favorite time of year. I loved the carnival and all the concessions on the midway. I even got to know some of the carnies that operated the rides.

When I was growing up, if someone had asked me what I wanted to be, I would have said I wanted to be the guy that operated the Ferris wheel. The fair lasted seven days. I sat in the grandstand and saw every show, from horse racing to the Grand Ole Opry. My dad became president of the fair board, which meant I could get free passes to some of the events. Those were the days.

One of my childhood friends was Skip Mallors, whose father owned both movie theaters in town. I never had to pay to see a movie, and that went for the popcorn too. Every time I watch an old movie on TV, it reminds me of home. Skip passed on a few years ago. That's one of the unfortunate things about getting to be eighty—you lose a lot of friends that you've known through the years.

Another event in my hometown was Kids Day where they always had a soapbox derby. One year my father and I spent the entire summer putting together a racer for the derby. It wasn't very streamlined, but believe it or not, I took second place. What a thrill! So my childhood wasn't cut short by dance and xylophone lessons. In fact, it made me sort of popular with the kids at school, and I was always performing for some sort of function.

My dad came from a large family, but my mother had only one brother, Lawrence, whom I was also named after. My full name is Lawrence Jack Imel. Uncle Lawrence's wife, Aunt Virginia, was a piano teacher, and she convinced Mom and Dad that if I wanted to be a musician I should study piano. She was right because the piano is the foundation for any instrument you may choose to play.

My Aunt Virginia was a sweetheart, extremely polite, with more patience than you could believe. I studied with her for about three years, and by the time I was ten years old, I had made progress with my dancing and knew several songs on the xylophone. Of course I was still performing to my old favorite "Bye Bye Blues."

My mother thought I should enter some amateur shows, which were very popular back in the 1940s. If you hoped to be discovered, that was a good way to find out how you stacked up against other performers and learn what the audience liked. They had judges who determined who won and who placed second and third. In a two-year span, I probably entered at least a dozen amateur shows. I'll tell you right now, I never won. I came in second or third a few times, but no cigar.

I had trouble understanding why some of these people won. One time I got beat by a guy who played songs on a blow torch, and the people loved it. You can bet a baton twirler would catch the judge's attention, along with any kid who could sing "Danny Boy" or "God Bless America," dressed up like Uncle Sam. But the one I remember most was a guy who had three pigs that sang "The Bells of St. Mary's." Let me explain. Each pig had an oink that could make a different sound. The guy would put his arms around the pig's neck and squeeze. The more he squeezed, the higher the oink. Somehow it came out sounding like "The Bells of St. Mary's," and he won hands down.

Every time I lost a contest, I went home and tried to improve myself. Plus, every time I entered a contest, I gained a little more experience. I always felt that when something goes wrong, it just makes you more determined. Eventually Mom thought it was time to replace the xylophone with a marimba.

The only difference between the two is that the marimba has wider keys and a much richer sound, with a lot of resonance.

It was around this time that I met Dorothy Durbin who owned a theatrical agency in Fort Wayne, and she's the one who really got me started in show business. She was always looking for new acts, so my parents set up an audition. I played three or four numbers on the marimba, and then for my finish, I danced and played at the same time. She seemed impressed, and a few weeks later gave me a booking at the CIO Union Hall. I was paid $25 for my first professional job, and believe me, that was good money in 1944. The show went well, and it wasn't long before Dorothy called me again for another date. The CIO Union wanted me back, and that's always a good sign.

Things got even better as the months went along. My bookings were usually on weekends, so they didn't interfere with my school lessons. I worked for Dorothy Durbin all through high school. This gave me confidence, and I was getting great experience at the same time. I made and saved enough money to get through at least two years of college; my parents never took a cent of the money I earned.

This was my bell boy costume.

My dad drove me all over the state of Indiana to play those dates, and he helped me carry the marimba parts up and down many stairways. Most of my engagements were for the Moose Club, the Elks Club, American Legion, and VFW. I especially appreciated the Moose and Elks Clubs because they would always ask me back. In fact, I later became a member of both organizations. I'll never forget the wonderful time I had working for Dorothy Durbin—she was the best. I probably would never have made a career in show business if it hadn't been for Mom and Dad and Dorothy Durbin.

Here I am dressed up as Uncle Sam.

I was an enthusiastic young patriot and always turned on the charm when I performed for service organizations.

Two

BASKETBALL DREAMS: PLAN B

In 1947 I was a 14-year-old freshman at Portland High. If you know anything about Indiana, it's probably the fact that high school basketball is the state's favorite sport. Every gym is packed on Friday and Saturday nights, and the most popular guys are the basketball players. Well, I was crazy about basketball. Every boy in Indiana played this game from the time he was old enough to walk, and I was no exception. I made the freshman team and practiced three days a week after school.

At this time, I was still taking marimba lessons from Jack Kurkowski. Unfortunately, one of the basketball practice days fell on the same day as my lesson. This was the first time that anything had ever made me to want to give up marimba lessons. It created big problems between me and my parents. I wanted to play basketball more than anything in the world, even more than marimba or tap dancing. I was really down on my parents, making things very unpleasant at home.

Finally my dad went to the coach, who confided that I had just barely made the team. My chances for a future as a varsity basketball player at Portland High were pretty slim. The coach told Dad he should have a talk with me. Well, he did and explained that I was too slow and too short. What a disappointment. A few days went by, and the coach called me into his office. He told me that very few boys who play basketball in high school are able to make a living at it later. He said I might have a better future if I stuck with my music and dancing.

After much thought, I finally came to realize that the coach was right. Portland High School had about 450 pupils, but the band was relatively small. In fact, there were only a dozen or so members, and their uniforms consisted only of caps. I certainly didn't think there would be any place for a marimba, but I went to see the band director, Mrs. Moore, anyway. She asked if I had ever played the drums. Believe it or not, they only had a bass drummer. There was a snare drum in the band room closet, so I told her I would take it home and see if I might be interested in playing it.

The marimba uses the same wrist action as the drums. I couldn't believe it. I took to it like a duck takes to water. I could read music, so it wasn't long before I was able to read drum parts. Mrs. Moore accepted the way I played and put me in the band.

Then in the summer of 1948, Mrs. Moore left, and the school board hired a new band director by the name of Rush Hughes. Did you ever see *The Music Man?* Well, Rush Hughes must have. That summer he raised money for instruments and uniforms, and by fall, the band went from twelve members to more than a hundred. Most of the students hadn't even taken lessons, but there they were in the band wearing full-dress uniforms. At the last football game of the season, the band marched out onto the field at halftime and played the school song. I often wondered how we sounded in the stands, but it didn't matter. Portland had a hundred kids in uniform playing in the high school band.

Funny, but Rush left town the next summer, and nobody ever heard from him again. There was talk after he disappeared that some money was missing from the donations account, but like I said, it was just talk. The next fall, they hired H. Paul Brown as the new band director. This guy really knew how to rehearse and conduct an orchestra, and he remained at the school until he retired.

During my senior year, a few of us formed a dance band. We used stock arrangements sold through any mail order or music store. We got together and rehearsed a couple of times a week. I even bought myself a set of used drums. Little did I know then that I'd be playing drums for the next sixty years.

I played drums with a group of friends in high school (back row left).

One of the guys in our band was a great trumpet player by the name of John Brigham. John could have been a professional musician, but his sights were set on the loan business, and he became very successful. John and I later joined the Navy together, and we have remained close friends all these years. He and his wife, Carol, have a home in Portland and another one in Florida where they spend their winters.

Playing drums in the dance band was great fun, and I have to say I came to enjoy that more than the marimba. But it's such a competitive instrument that even good drummers have trouble finding work at times, so the marimba and tap dancing always came first with me. Our group sounded pretty good, and we began getting dance jobs for school proms, sororities, even country clubs. However, my junior and senior years weren't as rosy as you might think.

My grades had been good enough through junior high, but I started to get a bad attitude during my junior year in high school. I was something of a clown to the other kids—anything for a laugh. I got kicked out of class more than once; I was even suspended for three days during my senior year. I was more interested in entertaining the other kids than I was in getting good grades. Being in the band was the only thing that was going right. I became a disappointment to my parents and teachers. I was still doing shows for Dorothy Durbin, but my school work was nothing to be proud of. My priorities were all wrong, and I knew it. I wasn't afraid of work, so when I wasn't doing shows for Dorothy, I was working in my dad's grocery store. Of course, I still found time to practice my music and dancing.

I used to help deliver groceries with my Uncle Roy, who was a real character. He drove the delivery truck, and my job was to take the groceries inside the house and put the things that needed to stay cold in the refrigerator; the rest went on the kitchen table. Now Uncle Roy liked his beer, and he knew which customers kept beer in their fridge. He would say to me, "Jack, I'll take this order in." Those were the people who always told Uncle Roy to help himself. What they didn't know was that eight or ten other customers had told him the same thing. We started around one in the afternoon and were through about three hours later. By four o'clock, I was really happy to see the back end of that grocery truck. Believe it or not, he never had an accident. I loved Uncle Roy—God bless him.

Getting back to school issues, my father met with the principal, and they agreed they should have a serious talk with me. I guess it worked because my grades started to improve, and I graduated without any problems.

Norma and I were in the high school band together. She also played the snare drum and was pretty good on it. She was my high school sweetheart, but I was not without some competition. Several other guys had their eyes on her too; one in particular was Junior May. He was president of my class and very popular. He also owned a new 1950 Buick. Very few kids had a car in those days. In fact, I didn't get my own car until I was out of school. Sometimes I could borrow my dad's car when I had a date with Norma, but I always worried about that guy with the fancy new car. Norma didn't like the way I clowned around in school and said I was a showoff. Whenever she got mad at me, she would go out with Junior. But he really was a nice guy, and we became friends in later years. As usual, Norma was right—I was a showoff.

After graduating from high school, I had to decide what I wanted to do with my life. Doing shows for Dorothy Durbin was fine, but limited. I mean, how much work was there for an act like mine around the Fort Wayne area? One thing for sure, I had gained a lot of experience working for Dorothy. I was learning how to work an audience and how to deal with some of the problems that come with being an entertainer.

Most of the time I used only a piano player for accompaniment, but sometimes I had a band, and I never knew how good they'd be. I didn't have charts, so I had to arrive at the job early enough to rehearse. The band had to be able to fake my music. I did have sheet music for the piano, but there were times when the piano player couldn't read music, and the other musicians couldn't fake it. So I just hoped for the best. If the piano player was okay, but the band wasn't, I used the piano along with the drummer. I had to be careful about the drummer too, because sometimes I'd end up with a guy who thought a beat was something you grow in a garden. It seems there was always some kind of problem with the sound. Some places didn't even have a mic, so if the audience was drinking, it was hard to get their attention. All these situations helped me to understand the business, but I wanted to learn more about music.

Some of my friends were going to Indiana University where my grandfather, a charter member of the Phi Gamma Delta fraternity, had studied medicine and graduated. My friend Bruce Klopfenstein was a Phi Gamma there, and he invited me to a rush party during late spring of 1950. If I handled myself right, I might get accepted into the fraternity.

So I drove to Bloomington for the pledge party. Man, I tell you, they watched every move I made. This affair lasted three days, and on the last day they had a picnic where they arranged dates for all the pledges. I was five feet eight inches, but my date was over six feet tall. How could I pretend to be interested in a girl who was a head taller than me? I was polite and remembered what my mother had taught me about manners. The fraternity brothers drove us to the picnic, and on the way back I fell asleep with my date right beside me. I don't even remember saying good night to her. Afterward, Bruce told me that my chances of becoming a Phi Gamma were pretty thin. He was right. I never heard from the fraternity again, but things usually turn out for the best.

Even though Indiana University had one of the largest music and theater arts departments in the country, I found out about an excellent marimba teacher at the Arthur Jordan Music Conservatory in Indianapolis, which is affiliated with Butler University. If I had gone to IU for four years, I would have earned a degree, but that wasn't really what I wanted. My main interest was to learn more about the marimba, so I ended up going to the Arthur Jordan Music Conservatory.

Chuck Henze taught the marimba, and he proved to be everything I'd heard and more. Not only was he a good teacher, but he was a great player as well. In addition to teaching, he performed with the Indianapolis Symphony. Chuck was a first-rate percussionist—drums, timpani, trap, xylophone—you name it, he could play it. I soon found myself practicing at least four or five hours a day. I really took the marimba seriously (not that I hadn't previously), but I started playing songs that I never thought I could play before. Of course there were other studies such as English, music appreciation, and sight reading, but I sure learned a lot from Chuck. I'd been at the Conservatory for about eight weeks when I heard that *The Horace Heidt Show* was coming to town, and my path took another turn.

Three

JACK'S GOT TALENT!

If you haven't heard the name Horace Heidt before, let me tell you about this famous bandleader. He led one of the most popular bands in the 1940s and early 1950s. Always looking for young new talent, he put together a Youth Opportunity Program that aired on the radio every Sunday night and even on early television. Horace Heidt toured the country doing one-nighters, and the winning talent would be featured on his radio and television shows. The winner advanced to the next week and remained until someone else came come along and won. His talent scouts selected four contestants in each town.

Talent shows had never been kind to me, and *The Horace Heidt Show* was no exception. When he came to Muncie in 1949, I auditioned for his talent scout, but once again, it was no cigar. I decided to try again the next year and went to Marion in hopes that my luck would change. After all, I knew I had improved from a year ago with all my practice at the Conservatory. Well guess what? The talent scout liked what I did and told me I would be a contestant. What a thrill it was to know that I'd be performing in front of Horace Heidt. And that was just the beginning.

I won the talent contest, and Heidt told my parents that he might find a place for me. I assumed that by winning in Marion, I would appear on his Sunday night radio show, but nothing more was said about it. Three weeks later, I received a telegram telling me to be in New York to join *The Horace Heidt Show*. As excited as I was, I couldn't help but wonder what I'd be doing on his show because he already had a blind marimba player and a tap dancer with a wooden leg. How in the world could I follow that?

I took the train from Portland to New York City and checked in at the Abbey Hotel, just a block from Times Square. What an unbelievable city! I walked around for hours. In 1950 Times Square seemed like a carnival, and there wasn't much crime back then. The next day I reported to Horace Heidt. He shook my hand and welcomed me to the show. I was about to find out just what he had in mind for me.

Heidt had a dance line of six boys and six girls, and I was going to replace one of the male dancers. They performed six numbers in the show, and I had to learn the steps from the wings. I could tell I wasn't too popular with the guy I was replacing. He could see me watching, but as they say, that's show biz. Even though I wouldn't be playing the marimba now, I believed that being with the show was going to help me in the future.

That's me performing on tour with the Horace Heidt Dancers (third from left).

Unfortunately, it meant I had to leave the Arthur Jordan Conservatory, and I would no longer be able to study with Chuck

Henze. It was November, and we would be on the road doing one-nighters until May. We were always either doing a show or traveling by car to the next city. Twelve cars carried the cast, and two trucks hauled wardrobe, instruments, and television and radio equipment. I didn't get so much as one day off for the next six months. But I was only eighteen years old, and I loved being part of the show.

We played every major city in the United States, starting from New York and ending at Horace Heidt's ranch in Van Nuys, California. All twelve cars were painted red, white, and blue. Heidt rode in a 1939 Cadillac, which at one time had belonged to President Roosevelt. Heidt always left earlier than the rest of us. When we spotted his car parked at the edge of the city we were heading for, we were supposed to stop, and then all twelve cars would parade through town, honking their horns.

Horace Heidt was a real showman and had a million gimmicks. He was a little like Lawrence Welk in that regard. He knew what the audience liked and how to give it to them. He wasn't a musician, but he knew what would please the public. Heidt had been a football player at Stanford until he got hurt one season and decided to become a bandleader. I guess he just wanted to be in front of the public.

Heidt had a blind marimba player by the name of Pierce Knox. He knew I played the marimba too, even though I didn't play it on the Heidt show. I asked Pierce if I could practice on his instrument once in a while when it didn't interfere with his schedule. He said to go ahead, but when I finished, be sure to put the mallets at the left end of the marimba. I promised I would always put them in the exact same place. I appreciated that because I could at least stay familiar with some of the exercises Chuck Henze had taught me.

A few nights, later Heidt introduced Pierce, and the band started playing his intro music. He reached for his mallets, but there were no mallets. I had put them on the right side of his instrument by mistake. Heidt saw the mallets and handed them to Pierce, but the damage had been done. I apologized, but I never played his instrument again after that. I felt terrible about the whole incident.

Our tour ended up in Van Nuys in April of 1951, and our country was at war with Korea. I was eighteen at the time, and boys my age were still getting drafted. I called my father, and he told me the draft board had contacted him—I would be called up in six months. My main concern was what would happen to my job with Horace Heidt, so I went to him and explained my situation.

He told me he was sorry, but the best thing for me was to go back to Portland and spend what few months I had left with my parents and friends. I realized he was right, so I left the show and went back to my hometown. I would miss all the people I had worked with, but at the same time, I could enjoy being home with my family, and of course, spending time with my sweetheart, Norma.

It was at this time that I met Jay Miller, and we have been close friends for over fifty years now. Jay has been a successful beer distributor in Portland. He still owns the business, but he turned most of the managing over to his son Ted. In fact, he did so well that he was able to bring the Budweiser Clydesdales to Portland twice. That company is very particular about where they send their beautiful horses, and only a few distributors have had that honor.

Jay played the tenor saxophone and thought we should form a dance band. There were some first-rate musicians in the area, so it sounded like a good idea, and it didn't take long to get started. We had John Brigham on first trumpet, who I mentioned became successful in the loan business; Richard Bibler on saxophone, who later became a bank president in Milwaukee; Bruce Klopfenstein on piano, who had tried to get me into the fraternity at Indiana University; Skip Mallors on saxophone and piano, whose father owned six theaters in and around the state of Indiana (we used him on piano when Bruce wasn't available); Paul Brown on saxophone, my high school band director; Dale Gagle on trombone, a student in the high school band; and a bass player.

We bought some stock arrangements and practiced at least once or twice a week. We called ourselves the Starlighters and were pretty good too. It wasn't long before we started getting dance jobs around the area. We got along well together and didn't really have a leader of the band. Brownie called the tunes, John Brigham counted off the band, and Rich Bibler was the treasurer. Yours truly was the drummer, and I was still able to practice my marimba and get some bookings from Dorothy Durbin in Fort Wayne.

Four

ANCHORS AWEIGH

I was still dating Norma, of course, but I had to think about the draft, which was coming up in January of 1952. I heard somewhere that if you were in the National Guard Band in Muncie you were exempt from the draft, so John Brigham and I tried out. We passed the audition, but found out later that you had to have been in the National Guard Band before June of 1951. So then John and I decided to join the Navy together. This meant I would be away for four years and would not be able to see much of Norma until my enlistment was up. However, joining the Navy would later turn out to be one of the best things that ever happened for me.

So it was "anchors aweigh" for John and me. We took the train from Indy to the Great Lakes Naval Training Center and were surprised to run into a friend of ours, Pete Brewster, on the train. Pete had been a basketball and football player at Portland High School. What an athlete! He made All State in basketball and was now playing on the Purdue football team. He became an All American in both sports at Purdue, and the team was traveling to play Northwestern. We rode together all the way to Chicago, and he introduced John and me to several of the Purdue players. He later went on to play for the Cleveland Browns for over ten years. Without a doubt, Pete Brewster was a football star, and Portland was very proud to be his hometown.

After the train ride, John and I reported for duty at the naval base, as boot camp was about to begin. We were in the same company, so we leaned on each other's shoulders and experienced the training together. As I think back, boot camp wasn't that bad. John laughed at some of the things we had to do, but I confess I didn't think that some of them were all that funny. Of course we were both homesick, and I certainly missed Norma. Another thing I missed was my music and tap dancing.

The Navy had what they called Smokers. It's a variety show made up of professional entertainers, but if any recruits had talent, they landed a spot on the show. I called my parents and asked if they could bring my marimba and tap shoes to the base, and as always, they said yes. They drove all the way from Portland to Illinois, but I was only allowed to talk with them for a short time. I unloaded the marimba and set it up in the barracks. Later that day, the company chief walked in and asked, "What the hell is that?"

I walked over to him and said, "That belongs to me. I want to try out for the Smokers."

I performed my tap-dancing marimba act at Navy Smokers.

He said okay, but I'd have to put it someplace else in another building. It ended up in a hangar, but that was fine. I passed the audition and performed in about four or five Smokers during boot camp. Chief Wonders was in charge of the Smokers, and he suggested that I try out for the Navy School of Music if I wanted to stay with my music. It was the only way I could be designated as a musician after boot camp. I had to audition for the chief, who was director of the Great Lakes Band. He thought my marimba playing was fine, but unfortunately it wasn't a military instrument.

"You can't march down the street playing a marimba," he said. Then he asked if I played the drums. I hadn't read any drum music since high school. He put some drum music in front of me and told me to sight read it. I failed the test, and the music school in Washington, DC, turned me down. I was heartbroken. If I had known about this requirement, I could have at least practiced a little beforehand. I hadn't held a pair of drumsticks since leaving Portland, so I just wasn't prepared.

Meanwhile, with only a few days left in boot camp, I was told I would be going to the supply depot in Pearl Harbor for duty. Well, that would be fine: two years of shore duty and then Norma and I could get married in Hawaii, but performing would have to wait.

Then I received good news from Chief Wonders. One thing about the military, your orders can change in a snap. He informed me that I would be staying at Great Lakes for the next two years, entertaining the recruits. The chain of command thought I would be more useful as a performer than at the supply depot in Hawaii.

My job included giving recruits a written test each day and holding auditions for the shows. I could hardly wait to tell Norma. It meant that I could spend most weekends in Portland, which was only 250 miles away. Conducting the written tests was an education for me too. There were a few recruits who couldn't read or write, so I had to read the questions to them, along with the three multiple-choice answers. Only about thirty percent passed. I felt bad for those who failed, but I had no choice. I had to grade them accordingly. Auditioning the recruits was a lot easier, and some of them really had a lot of talent. I did what I could by telling Chief Wonders which ones I thought were good enough to perform in the Smokers. The rest was up to him. I was able to get home a couple of weekends a month, but driving 250 miles was starting to seem more like 500.

I always ended my act with a flourish by leaping over the marimba.

Five

CHANCE OF A LIFETIME

I knew I would be at Great Lakes for at least two years, so Norma and I decided to get married. We had a small church wedding in the fall of 1952 and moved into an apartment in Waukegan, Illinois. Our marriage years were about to begin.

Our apartment was small, but I didn't care, as long as we were together. We had our first child, a boy, the following spring, and we named him Gregory Denney after Norma's maiden name. Our parents were proud.

My tour of duty at Great Lakes was coming to an end in the fall of 1954, and the location of my remaining two years in the service was not known. I was still doing Smokers twice a month, but that would soon be over. One of my last performances was with the famous banjo player Eddie Peabody, also a captain in the Navy Reserve, who was popular during the 1930s and 1940s.

We did the show together, and he seemed impressed. He asked me why I didn't go to the Navy School of Music. I explained that I didn't play a military instrument, and I couldn't read drum music well enough. Eddie Peabody said he might be able to help me. Well, he sure did. He called the music school, and they accepted me. This meant that I would go to Washington, DC, for nine months and then be assigned to a band. The only catch to this whole thing was that I would have to extend my enlistment by one year. Well, that was fine with me. One more year in the Navy was worth it to be designated as a musician. I was still a seaman, so I could at least make third class before my enlistment was up. You can call it fate, luck, or just being at the right place at the right time. I still had four to five weeks left before I started at the music school, so I really got into my drums, especially the sight reading. I practiced day and night.

Norma and I found a new apartment, larger than the one in Waukegan, because our family was bigger now that we had our son, Gregory. Of all the cities we ever lived in, I think Washington, DC, was our favorite. Things were going good at the school, and I was holding my own on the drums. I even got to do my marimba and tap dancing act in some of the officers' clubs.

After one show I was approached by a Mr. Alex Sheftell, who was in charge of advertising for ABC Television in Washington, DC. Before that, he had been advertising manager for Jackie Gleason. He asked me if I would be interested in having a manager. I explained that the work would be limited since I was in the service, but that didn't seem to bother him. Alex assured me, "It's in the bag, Jack." He had connections in New York as well as DC and could get me an audition for a television show in New York that was seen on the ABC network. What did I have to lose? I agreed to at least an audition. Most of my weekends were free, so he set it up, and we took the train to New York.

The show was called *Chance of a Lifetime*, hosted by Dennis James, a well-known TV personality at that time. It was like an amateur show, but if you won, you received $1,000 and a week's booking at the Latin Quarter in New York City. You would also be on the TV show the next week, and these appearances continued until you were beaten out by someone else. Well, I passed the audition, and the fact that I was in the Navy didn't bother the producers at all. In fact, they thought it would create even more public interest. The Navy School of Music thought so too and gave me the okay. So I got to appear on a TV show that was seen from coast to coast.

Norma, our son, and I joined Alex "It's-in-the-bag-Jack" Sheftell and headed for the Big Apple. My biggest competition was a young singer named Diahann Carroll, but at least it was a chance to be seen all over the country. The outcome was decided by an applause meter. It was close, but Diahann won by only three or four ticks.

Norma was more disappointed than I was; just being on the show had been a plus, and that was enough to convince me that Alex would make a good manager. I signed a contract with him, strictly on a ten-percent basis. Incidentally, Diahann Carroll went on to become a recording star, a movie actress, and a big hit on Broadway.

Alex booked me at the Shoreham Hotel in Washington for two weeks, plus a few other engagements in the area. Then one night he called with some good news. The *Chance of a Lifetime* TV show wanted to give me another chance. It seems that a lot of viewers thought I should have won. Apparently the applause for me had actually been more than what registered on the meter. So we went back to New York and gave it another go.

This time I competed with Tommy Leonetti, who later became a singing star on the TV show *Your Hit Parade*. This was going to be a real challenge, and I knew it. But things went well for me that night, and I won. Alex, Norma, and I were beside ourselves. I won $1,000, but unfortunately, I couldn't accept the week's booking at the Latin Quarter because of my Navy schedule. But that was all right because winning that contest really boosted my confidence.

Since Alex and I had an extra day to spend in New York, he asked if I would like to see *The Jackie Gleason Show*. Afterward he would take me backstage to meet "The Great One" himself. Of course, I was excited; he'd always been one of my favorites. Alex and I spent the entire day at the theater watching the rehearsal and broadcast of Gleason's opening show for the season. What a master he was! It's a day I'll never forget.

True to his word, Alex took me backstage after the show. It sounded like Gleason and his production staff were somewhat unhappy about the performance because I could hear them arguing in the dressing room. I thought we should forget about seeing him, but Alex knocked on the door anyway. Gleason's manager answered the door, and we walked in. He seemed happy to see Alex, even though there was an apparent disagreement taking place.

Alex said, "Jackie, there's a young man here I'd like you to meet. He has a lot of talent."

Gleason had a towel wrapped around his neck. He looked at me and said, "What did you think of the show, kid?"

I was pretty nervous, but I answered, "I thought the show was great."

Gleason turned to his production staff and said, "See there, he liked it."

Alex said he knew Gleason was busy, but he wanted him to watch me on *Chance of a Lifetime*, which was going to air the following week.

I thought Alex was overdoing our welcome, but Gleason said, "I'll make sure one of my staff people takes a look."

Alex said goodbye, and we left. I was thrilled about meeting Gleason, although I felt we had imposed on him. But that was the way Alex worked, and I was impressed.

It was time to think about what I should do for my third appearance on *Chance of a Lifetime*. I worked up a new routine and gave it to the arranger Milton Delugg. He was well-known in the music business and on staff with *Chance of a Lifetime*. Until now, singers had been my competition, but this time I was going up against a novelty act, a guy who played a cigar box. That's right. It looked like a violin, but the body part was nothing more than a single string across a cigar box, and he could play songs on it. Well, the audience must have thought he was pretty good because he won. It would have been nice to win another $1,000, but it wasn't meant to be.

When I was a kid, I had lost to three singing pigs, then to a guy who played a blow torch, and now to a guy plucking a cigar box. But the audience thought he was great, and that's what counts in show biz. At least I had made three appearances on a coast-to-coast show.

When I returned to the music school, everyone thought I got robbed, but I'm afraid they were a bit partial. A few weeks later, I was watching *The Jackie Gleason Show*. He always featured The June Taylor Dancers who opened the show. Well, they did a routine that blew my mind. The girls all tap danced and played miniature xylophones at the same time. Yes, I guess Gleason did watch *Chance of a Lifetime* after all. That's when I learned that nothing is sacred in show business.

With two weeks left at the Navy School of Music, I received my orders right before graduation. I was assigned to a band in San Diego where I would spend the next two and a half years, and that would complete my enlistment. I took two weeks' leave and prepared to head for California with Norma and Greg.

Before we left, I noticed in the newspaper that my ex-boss Horace Heidt was appearing at the Biltmore, so I paid him a visit just to say hello. Well, he was more than happy to see me. He told me that his solo tap dancer had just left the show and asked if I would be interested in returning for a four-week tour. Heidt was leaving town the same day that I was starting my leave. He was doing a series of one-nighters across the country that would end in California. I told him that I'd love to accept, but I was in the Navy. Heidt didn't bat an eye. He said that was no problem; he would work something out.

Well, I don't know who he talked to or who he knew in Washington, DC, but my orders were changed to report to the band in San Diego after a four-week tour with Horace Heidt. Norma and Greg flew back to Portland to visit family and would meet me in St. Louis, two weeks into the tour. I drove my own car, and Heidt paid for my gas. One of his entertainers, Dick Kerr, rode with me. He was a great entertainer and fun to have as a traveling companion. That was in 1955. Dick and I stayed friends and kept in contact with each other until he died in 2010.

Norma and Greg joined me in St. Louis, and we all rode together to Van Nuys, where the tour ended. We had a great time, but now I had to report for duty in San Diego. Norma had packed my sea bag when she was back home in Indiana. On the first morning when I got dressed to report for duty, I discovered that I had two right shoes and no hat. So I showed up hatless, wearing two right shoes. When I came to attention, both my feet pointed to the left. It was two weeks until the next payday, so I would have to wear those two right shoes until then.

After about a week, the band master said, "Jack, this is hurting me more than it is you. Here's twenty bucks. Go buy yourself a pair of shoes and you can pay me back later."

It took a couple of months before I finally convinced the band that I wasn't a nut case. It was good duty, and the band was made up of talented musicians. Every morning we reported to a destroyer tender and performed. Next we went ashore to a band room where we practiced, and then back to the ship at noon to play a concert. We spent the rest of the day in the band room. We also played a concert once a week at the Navy hospital. This was 1955, and I'm happy to say that Norma and I had our second child, a baby girl we named Debra Lynn. So now we had two kids in our growing family, Greg and Debbie.

There are eleven naval districts in the Navy, and every year each one holds a talent contest. The first- and second-place winners go on to New York for a competition to determine the All-Navy winner and two runners-up. Ten of the contestants are picked to be on *The Ed Sullivan Show*, one of the top programs on television at the time. So I entered for the 11th District and came in first. Then I went to New York where I competed against twenty-one other acts. I took first place again and was picked to appear on *The Ed Sullivan Show*—1955 was a good year for me.

I won the Navy Talent Contest while attached to the Navy Band in San Diego.

Nathan Poole, a talent agent in San Diego, booked me from time to time. He told me that he needed three acts to fill in with an up-and-coming country singer by the name of Elvis Presley. Presley was fast becoming the biggest personality in show business. The show had to be two and a half hours, but Presley, who was a young overnight sensation, did not have enough material to go that long. So the three acts would go on during the first half, and then Presley and his band would do the rest. I told Nate I would be thrilled to be on the same show with Elvis Presley. Afterward I had a chance to talk with him backstage, and he was really down to earth. In fact, Elvis told me that he liked my work and hoped we might work together again sometime. I gave him my address in San Diego, and believe it or not, I received a Christmas card from him every year after that. Performing with Elvis was another night I'll always remember.

In 1956 I entered the All-Navy Talent Contest again. I repeated as winner of the 11th Naval District, but this time I came out second in New York. However, I was picked to be on *The Ed Sullivan Show* again. What great experiences I had performing in New York, meeting Jackie Gleason, and being on *Chance of a Lifetime*. New York had been good to me, and none of this would have happened if I hadn't joined the Navy—and there was still more to come.

I'll never forget one engagement I had at a strip joint in National City, a border town just a few miles from Tijuana, Mexico. It was 1955, and I was still in the Navy. I worked there from September through New Year's Eve, five nights a week and two shows a night for $25 a night. Those strippers were so bad that I was the one who always closed the show. I mean, when a tap dancer and marimba player goes over better than a stripper in a strip joint, it doesn't say much for the strippers. There was only one dressing room for all of us, and sometimes the girls would change right in front of me. They acted like I wasn't even there.

One night a stripper was so drunk that I had to help her on with the costume she was going to take off on stage. Believe me, she looked better with her clothes on. They always kept the front door open, and between shows one night, a stray dog wandered in and lay down under a table. When I came out and hit the marimba, the dog jumped out from under the table, growling and showing his teeth. For a moment there, it looked like a wild animal act. From then on, I always checked under the tables.

They changed strippers every week, and one time they booked a female impersonator. Most of the time those guys were gay, but this one was straight. He arrived at the club dressed like a girl and even used the women's bathroom. I decided to have some fun with a couple of my Navy buddies. They knew I worked in a strip joint and constantly asked me if any of the girls were swingers. One time I told them, "Man, there's a girl this week that's really a knockout, and she digs sailors." I said I would introduce them to her after the show.

They came to the club with high expectations. I told the female impersonator to really play it up with my buddies. He had them all worked up until he took off his bra. I thought those guys were going to kill me, but it ended up being a lot of fun.

The owner of the club asked me if I could wait until the last two weeks of December to get paid and said he would give me a check on New Year's Eve. I told him that was fine; I didn't have any reason to doubt his honesty. When I asked for my check after the second show on New Year's Eve, he told me to take my marimba and get the hell out. I never got paid, but at least I learned a lesson. I found out later that this guy had been in prison. I couldn't go to the Musicians' Union because a serviceman wasn't supposed to work while he was in the military, even if he did belong to the union.

Six

YOU'RE HIRED!

In January of 1957, my discharge was fast approaching. Alex Sheftell, my manager, set up a contract for me with General Artists Corporation, but the contract didn't actually guarantee me any work. I had gained a pretty good reputation with the Navy, and they wanted me to join the Navy Band in Washington. It was very tempting. I would automatically be ranked to chief, spend my entire Navy career in Washington, and retire at the age of forty. However, I knew I would only go so far in show business being in the military, and I had much higher dreams.

My parents kept telling me I should try out for *The Lawrence Welk Show*. I really didn't know much about it because I had a steady gig on Saturday nights in an officers' club, the same night that the Welk Show was on TV. The entertainment office in San Diego informed me they had received a memorandum from the Welk people saying that anyone with talent could send them a tape for a chance to do a guest spot on his show. I had recorded a few numbers on the marimba in the music school, so I figured what do I have to lose? I sent in my tape and received a phone call from Les Kaufman on the Welk staff. They had listened to my recordings and wanted me to come to the Aragon Ballroom in Santa Monica so Welk could hear me play in person. If he liked what I did, I might get a guest spot on the show. This happened just two weeks before I was to be discharged. What an opportunity.

Welk was rehearsing his television show when I arrived, so I set up my marimba and patiently waited for my tryout. He finally walked over to me with that charm of his and asked if I was ready to play something with the band. I passed out a few charts to the musicians and flew into an arrangement called "After You've Gone."

I couldn't believe his reaction. Welk was jumping up and down, clapping his hands. The next number was "Bye Bye Blues," where I played and danced at the same time. He went out of his mind.

I had no doubt that he would give me a spot on his show. As I was packing up my marimba, he came over to me, eating a jar of baby food. Apparently he had a stomach condition and was very careful about his diet. Between the baby food and his accent, I must admit it was hard for me to keep a straight face. He asked me how much longer I had in the Navy, and I told him two weeks.

"We don't have the instrument you play in the band," he said, hinting that he might have a place for me. I almost fell to the floor. But then he added that he wasn't sure about hiring me. He would have to talk it over with his production staff, but he wanted me to at least make an appearance on his television show. I was overwhelmed with joy. I could hardly wait to get home to tell Norma and call my parents. I couldn't believe this was happening. Before I left the ballroom, Welk said, "Make sure you wear your uniform."

I floated home on cloud nine. The following week I drove to the ABC studio in Hollywood. When I walked in, I still couldn't believe this was happening. I rehearsed with the band on camera that morning, and everything went fine. The rest of the day I spent watching them rehearse the TV show. Everyone was nice to me, and I got a lot of compliments from the crew; however, nothing was said to me about being hired. But I felt it was an honor just to be making an appearance on his show.

At that time, the Welk Show was rated in the top ten. It was broadcast live in those days, and I was nervous, to say the least. I performed twice that night. First was "After You're Gone," and in the second half I played my old standby "Bye Bye Blues." Remember, we were performing live.

Welk walked up to me after my second number and said, "Jack, that was great. I understand you are getting out of the Navy in a couple of weeks, and then I'd like for you to report to me because, as of tonight, you are a member of the Champagne Music Makers."

Well, here again I couldn't believe this was happening to me. Norma, my parents, and friends—in fact, the whole country—was watching me be hired right there on live television. It was the happiest night of my life. My dreams and prayers were answered on January 7th of 1957. I had also been offered a position with the Navy Band in Washington, and I must say I gave that some thought. I would have to get out of my contract with Alex and General Artists Corporation, but in the end, I made the right choice.

I gave Lawrence Welk a marimba lesson.

I spent the next twenty-five years with Lawrence Welk and was with him until he retired in 1982. After that, I continued to perform with the Welk Stars. Lawrence, members of the band, and the singers were a wonderful group of people and made me feel right at home. Lawrence always referred to them as his Musical Family, and he was right: We all felt close to each other like a family.

Norma and I moved into an apartment in Van Nuys, and in March we were blessed with a second baby boy, Timothy Jack. So now we had three children: Gregory, Debbie, and Tim. How good does it get—a new job and a new baby boy?

I had been on the Welk Show for about two months when I suddenly realized that I was running out of material. I had been an act all my life, practicing and playing the same numbers for years. But now with television, I had to come up with something new every week. I worried that the numbers wouldn't be good enough, especially for a show that was on the network and live. I started to panic some.

My mother played the ukulele, and when I was a kid, she taught me how to play and sing a song called "Yes, Sir, That's my Baby." It was rather easy because the song had only three or four chord changes. Well, I remembered that, so I went out and bought myself a ukulele. I came up with a routine where I played and sang and then ended with a tap dance. When I went to rehearsal, Lawrence asked me where my marimba was. I told him that I had worked up a number with the ukulele.

"You mean to tell me you can play a ukulele?" He stopped the rehearsal and had everyone come up around the bandstand.

"Jack not only plays the marimba and tap dances," he said, "but he can play the ukulele too, and he's going to play it for you right now."

Well, that was the worst performance you ever heard. Lawrence stopped me after about eight bars. "Go on with the rehearsal," he told the others, "and Jack, you come down here." He was sitting at a table. "Sit down here, Jack. I want to talk to you about something."

He took a pencil and paper and drew up a chart from one hundred down to zero. "If I let you do the number you just showed me on my television show, where would you rate it on this chart?"

I knew it was pretty bad, so I said, "Well, maybe about a thirty."

"No," he said, and turned the paper over. Then he wrote minus ten, minus twenty, and so on until he ran out of paper. He made a mark at the bottom and said, "That's where I'd rate it."

So I confessed to him that I didn't have any more numbers that I thought were good enough to play on his show.

He said he had hired me because of my marimba playing. "Jack, everything you play doesn't have to be fast and furious. Play something slow and soft. We'll put a nice arrangement behind it, and it'll be fine. Make it simple."

I went home that night and told Norma what had happened. "Do what he says," she told me. "Come up with something slow and easy."

I took her advice and found some numbers that were easier and would cause less pressure on me. I hoped the public would understand and enjoy them. If I learned anything from Lawrence, it was simplicity. Keep it simple.

In September of 1957, we moved into a new house in Canoga Park that was about twenty miles from our old apartment. One day Lawrence called and said he had something he wanted to discuss with me. I immediately drove to his office with no idea what he wanted to talk about. He was sitting at his desk and greeted me with a warm handshake. He had a smile on his face, but I could tell something was wrong.

"Jack, we have been receiving some unfavorable mail about you. I wouldn't worry about it, but at the same time, I think you should read some of these letters and evaluate them in the hopes that we can win these people over."

He took me into another room and showed me a box about two feet high and two feet wide with my name on it. It was full of mail from people who didn't like my part of the show. In fact, some of them actually hated what I did. It was most disturbing, to say the least.

Fan mail was very important to Lawrence. He hired several girls who did nothing but answer the mail. Hundreds of letters were sent to the Welk office each week. A chart came out once a month with everyone's name on it that had two columns, one favorable and one unfavorable. Lawrence thought it was better to have ten favorable and no unfavorable than to have twenty-five favorable and two or three unfavorable.

Lawrence came back into the room where I was reading the letters. He looked at me and said, "Don't worry too much. Whenever I hire someone new, my audience thinks they're going to see less of their favorites. But I think I know what the problem is. Some of our fans don't think of you as part of the band. You seem to be more of a soloist than a member of the orchestra."

Each time I did a number, someone rolled my marimba out in front of the band. Since Lawrence had never had a marimba player before, there weren't any parts for me to play. When they featured the band doing an instrumental, you never saw me.

"You've got to do something with the band until parts can be written for you," Lawrence told me.

Most of the letters had accused me of being a showoff, saying I thought I was better than the rest of the guys in the band. On the contrary, I thought I was the poorest musician Lawrence had.

"Jack," he went on, "I was at a recording session the other day, and they had a fella who played a kitchen stool. He gave the recording a good feel, and the stool had a great sound." Lawrence reached into his pocket and handed me fifty dollars.

"I want you to go to a furniture store and buy two kitchen stools. Bring them to the studio, and George and I will decide which one has the best sound." George Cates was our musical director.

I felt pretty stupid going into the furniture store to buy a stool with a good sound, but Lawrence was the boss, so if I had to do this, I figured I'd have some fun with it. I put a pair of drumsticks in my inside coat pocket and walked into a furniture store. A sales clerk greeted me and asked if there was anything he could do for me.

"Yes," I answered. "Do you have any kitchen stools?"

They did, and we went to the back of the store where they had quite a variety.

"We have some with a small ladder and others that have a top you can turn."

"None of that is necessary," I interrupted. "I'm looking for a stool with the right sound." And with that, I pulled out my drumsticks and started beating on the top of the stools.

"Hey, what are you doing there?" the clerk asked. "We don't allow people to hit the furniture."

I ignored him and kept beating on the stools. He left and came back with the manager.

"What do you think you're doing here?"

"I'm looking for a stool with good sound, and if I find one, I'm going to play it on *The Lawrence Welk Show*."

Well, with that, the manager headed for the telephone. I stopped him and pulled out the fifty dollars.

"Don't call the police, I'm telling you the truth," I said. "I'm serious. I want to buy two stools."

I finally convinced him that I was on the level. I bought the stools, and on the way out, I told him to watch *The Lawrence Welk Show*. I took the stools to the studio and presented them to George Cates and Lawrence. I first played on one stool, then the other. I kept going back and forth until they finally decided which one they liked the best. I set it on the bandstand and placed it behind the drums. They put a microphone on it, and we got a sound check. Would you believe it? That night I played the kitchen stool during one of the instrumentals; they even gave me an eight-bar solo. I continued playing that stool for almost two years.

My dad called me one night and said, "A lot of people here in Portland are trying to tell me that you're playing a kitchen stool in the band. I told them they were crazy, but Jack, what is that thing you're beating on?"

"Dad, they're not crazy, that is a kitchen stool."

"Well, if that's what Lawrence wants you to play, then you play it."

For sure, I agreed with him. Not long after I started playing that stool, the bad mail stopped coming. The letters were now favorable, and the viewers came to accept me. Never in a million years did I ever dream that people would accuse me of being conceited or thinking I was better than the rest of the guys in the orchestra just because I played the marimba in front of the band. You have to be careful how you present yourself on television.

The public can be very opinionated. It took a person like Lawrence to come up with an answer that solved the problem, all because he really knew his audience. Pretty soon he started writing parts for me on things like bells and chimes, even marimba parts. From then on the mail was okay.

SEVEN

THE WELK FAMILY

Lawrence Welk was a master at choosing people who fit into his style of music and format. When I joined the band, it was self-contained. Guys like Rocky Rockwell had multiple talents. He was a great trumpet player with a flair for comedy and sang songs that had humor.

Then there was Larry Hooper, a fine piano player with a unique, deep bass voice. He recorded a song with Lawrence that became a hit in the fifties called "Oh, Happy Day." Dick Dale was a handsome fellow who could sing about any kind of song: ballad, country, and duets with Alice Lon, the Champagne Lady. But he was also one of the most versatile musicians in the reed section, playing soprano, alto, and baritone sax, and flute, and he could read anything you put in front of him.

Bob Lido sang tempo songs and played jazz violin. Aladdin, also played violin and sang in several different languages, which worked well for production numbers. All of these people had the right look about them and were perfect for television. They could handle any material they were given.

I've often been asked what made Lawrence Welk so successful. Well, you couldn't answer that with just a few words. He did so many things that made his television show a big hit for years. First of all, he had great instincts. The Lennon Sisters were one of his most popular attractions. He brought them on when they were little girls and made stars out of them. We discovered talents even they didn't know they had. I did a soft-shoe dance with Janet, and it was amazing how fast she caught on. All of the girls could turn on the charm, and it was a real treat for me whenever I worked with them, especially on a production number.

Lawrence loved Dixieland music, and he found a gem when he hired Pete Fountain. He was one of the best, if not the best, clarinet players I have ever heard. Pete and I joined the band at the same time in 1957. We drove to work together, and he was a barrel of laughs. We have stayed friends all these years.

Lawrence always surrounded himself with good talent and was careful about the people he hired. Besides talent, they had to be easy to get along with and appreciate the job. The orchestra was a real family.

In 1959 Norma gave birth to our fourth child, a baby girl named Cynthia Diane. A year later, we had our fifth and last child, Terrence Mark. So I had quite a family: Greg, Debbie, Tim, Cindy, and now Terry. It was getting a little crowded around the house, so in 1964 we moved into a bigger one that would be our home for the next thirty-five years.

One of my best friends was Joe Feeney, the Irish tenor from Grand Island, Nebraska. He had nine kids, and we hit it off good. Our families always got together on holidays, especially Christmas. That was really something to see, all of our kids, fourteen to be exact, in the same house. Joe and I went everywhere together. After Pete Fountain left the show, Joe and I took turns driving to work with each other since we lived only a few miles apart in Canoga Park. His wife, Georgia, and Norma were good friends, so we had a lot of fun times together. Joe and I were roommates when the band went on the road.

I should mention that when I joined the show, I was given a new automobile. Dodge was our sponsor, and everyone on the Welk Show received a new car from them every year. We all parked our cars together at the Aragon Ballroom, which was quite a sight to see: twenty-five new Dodges parked in front of the ballroom. It was good advertising for the Dodge Corporation. One year all the cars were the same color. When we left after work, it was confusing for everyone, trying to figure out which car was theirs. We finally put our names in the back window so we could tell the difference.

Our schedule was pretty much the same every year. We did thirty-two live shows, and then twenty of them were later shown as reruns during the summer when we went on tour. Each tour was usually ten towns in ten days, always major cities. Lawrence said that our TV ratings always improved in the cities after we played there.

The venues held anywhere from 12,000 to 20,000 people, and we filled them almost every time. Sometimes we would play big arenas and universities like Notre Dame, Texas, and Oklahoma. We also played some of the big state fairs. We traveled by air, so we were limited as to the amount of equipment we could carry. Our biggest challenge was the sound equipment. Technology in the 1950s and 1960s was pretty basic. The quality of mics and speakers was terrible at times, especially at fairs and arenas. The arenas were designed for sports events, so if you didn't have your own sound system, it could be a real problem.

Lawrence didn't want the expense of hauling a sound system to every city because they were all one-nighters and hundreds of miles apart. Transporting a sound system by air would have cost a fortune. It was surprising how well the concert went in a building that was used mainly for basketball. The stage was set up at one end of the floor, which meant there were seats behind us where the audience saw only the back of our heads. They were warned when they bought their tickets, but they bought them anyway. That is how popular the Welk Show was. People just wanted to see what we looked like in person. We always made an effort to sign autographs and shake hands with the folks who had those seats.

Along with the fairs and one-nighters, we had an engagement every summer at Harrah's in Lake Tahoe. This was special. Bill Harrah, who owned the casino, loved *The Lawrence Welk Show*, and we played three weeks there every June for seventeen straight years. The working conditions were great, with first-class sound and lighting and beautiful dressing rooms. It was sort of a vacation for all of us, and Bill Harrah treated us well. Everything in the casino was free to us except for the gambling.

Mr. Harrah liked us so much that he even built a special room onto his home to entertain all the Welk people with dinner and cocktails while we were there.

EIGHT

THE IMEL FAMILY

As I look back over all my years, I realize that the important thing is not what I might have accomplished, but my relationship with God and my family. Our first child, Gregory, was born in Waukegan, Illinois, while I was stationed there in the Navy. The service had strange rules back then. When your wife went to the hospital to have a baby, the husband was not allowed to go in and be with her. This seemed odd to me, but I drove Norma to the hospital and dropped her off. "See you later."

I had to keep calling to ask if the baby had been born yet. Norma was in labor for more than two days, so I had a long wait. (So did she, I might add.) When I finally got the call, I hurried to the hospital to see my son and wife. Being an only child myself, I had never seen a newborn baby before, and it was quite a shock for me. Because Norma had been in labor so long, the baby's skin was all dried out and wrinkled, like a little old man. I looked at him and thought, "This is my son?"

I left the hospital and drove to Portland to pick up my mom who was going to help with the baby when Norma came home. After a few days and a lot of baby lotion, Greg finally started to look like a real baby, and I felt like a real dad. I couldn't believe it—I had a family.

We took Greg everywhere with us. The Chicago Theater always had a live stage show between movies. It wasn't really the place for a baby, but we never hired a babysitter for him. He was very good, so we always took him along. Sometimes we went to Portland on weekends. Dorothy Durbin, the agent in Ft. Wayne, could usually book me someplace on a Saturday night, and the grandparents would take care of Greg. If I didn't do a show, we went out with our friends. Sunday night we would drive back to the base. Sometimes we left so late that I barely made it in time to report for duty. Oh, what you can do when you're young.

When I was stationed in San Diego, we always spent our summer vacations in Indiana. Gregory was our mischievous little boy who loved to pick on his baby sister. He would grab her pacifier and replace it with a sucker. In those days, a milkman delivered milk to our house. One morning we noticed that Greg was missing, and we went into a panic. Where could he be? Just then the milk truck came up the street with Greg sitting on the driver's lap. Greg had climbed into the back of the truck and stowed away while our milk was being delivered. After that, whenever I was outside washing my car or working in the yard, I put him on a leash and tied it to the front of the garage. Nowadays that would probably be called child abuse, but back then I just needed to know where he was.

Our third baby was due in March, so Norma's mother came, and this time there would be no Navy rules or regulations. Norma had planned to go to a private maternity hospital not far from our apartment, and I was looking forward to being there when the baby was born. But the very day she went into labor, I came down with chicken pox. Norma's mother drove her to the hospital and was with her for the birth of our son Timothy Jack. This was not what I had planned, but Tim was perfect, and that was the main thing. As I look back on 1957, it was the most amazing year of my life, filled with so many blessings. At the time, I didn't even realize how lucky I was. I had a great job, a new baby, and a brand new car from the Dodge organization. We bought our first home and put in a swimming pool. Life was good!

Two years went by and we were expecting our fourth child, so Norma's mother was with us again to watch the other children. However, she could only stay for two weeks, and Norma was now past her due date. When we explained our situation to the doctor, he said he would induce labor. Well, Norma was happy about that because then we could plan the delivery for a time when I wasn't filming the show. The doctor scheduled her for 6:30 p.m. on a Wednesday after he was finished seeing his other patients. I had previously agreed to do a show for the Boy Scouts on that same afternoon, but thought for sure I would be done by six. Since my performance was in Van Nuys, not far from the hospital, I would just meet Norma there.

Of course, shows don't always run on time. It was an awards luncheon, and I wasn't scheduled to perform until after the ceremony. I never expected so many awards to be given out—and so many speakers. By the time I came on, I knew I probably wouldn't make it in time. I finished my show and said, "You've been a wonderful audience, but my wife is in labor, and I have to leave." That remark got more applause than my act did.

I hurried into the hospital, but by then they were ready to wheel Norma into the delivery room. The doctor gave me a dirty look, "I thought we planned this time so you would be here." There was nothing for me to say. We had another baby girl and named her Cynthia Diane.

Ten months later, we were expecting our fifth child, and I had a show in Orange County that was two hours away from home. But Norma wasn't due for another two weeks, and her mother was already on the way by train from Indiana. I never considered the possibility that Norma might go into labor early, but she did. Remember, there were no cell phones back then. When I got home at three in the morning, she met me with "I'm in labor, we've got to get to the hospital right now." We called and woke up a neighbor to come stay with the children, and I raced all the way to the hospital.

"How long is this going to take?" I asked. "You know I've been up all night." As soon as the words came out of my mouth, I realized I'd said the wrong thing—and she has never let me forget it. Terrence Mark was born a few minutes after we arrived.

That was it, the end of having babies. We had our big family and were both young enough to have fun with all of them. I was twenty-eight and had been with the Welk Show for three years. I felt very blessed.

NINE

ALL I WANT FOR CHRISTMAS

Through the years, the Christmas show was always one of the most popular Welk productions. All the Welk people introduced their wives or husbands and children on camera, and the audience was as interested in our families as they were in us. If any of the youngsters had talent, they could perform on the show, usually with their mother or father, but occasionally by themselves. Some played instruments, and others sang or danced.

Our six-year-old daughter Debbie was taking ballet and tap lessons. She was pretty good, so I thought it might be cute to work up a tap dance that we could do together. She would be dressed like a doll with a key on her back, and I'd be Jack-in-the-Box. After I sprang out of the box to wind her up, we'd perform a tap routine. We spent a lot of hours rehearsing, and the hard work paid off because we performed it on the Christmas show. The scene was set up as a toy shop, with our other children, Greg, Tim, Cindy, and Terry, sitting on props like a horse or a toy car, watching the dance. Lawrence commented on camera, "That was a cute number," and we received quite a bit of favorable mail.

The following September, I came up with an idea for a number I could do with all of my children to the song, "Parade of the Wooden Soldiers." The setting was again a toy shop with all six of us dressed like toy soldiers who come to life. I could teach the boys some kind of drum kicks, with Greg on the snare drum, Tim on bass drum, and Terry playing the cymbals. I taught Debbie and Cindy a couple of dance steps they could do with me.

I had three months to prepare, and by December we were ready to show the act to Lawrence. Greg sounded good on the snare, Tim had a nice steady beat on the bass drum, and Terry wasn't a bit timid about clanging the cymbals. Debbie had her steps down perfect, and Cindy really showed a lot of personality. At the rehearsal, I went over the music and routine with Bob Smale. I couldn't believe how well the kids did when we showed the number to Lawrence. He was impressed and told the children they could perform it on the Christmas show. Norma and I were so proud of them.

It was a memorable night for the Imel children when they performed with Dad in the Parade of the Wooden Soldiers on a Welk Christmas Show.

On the day of the show, we rehearsed on camera with the band. My biggest concern was whether they could keep time with the band and not be afraid of the cameras. The run-through and the dress rehearsal both went well, and then we had one last time to practice the number. The kids didn't show any outward signs of being nervous—the only nervous one was me. They really charmed the audience, and afterward everyone told them how well they did. Norma was thrilled, and I could see a tear or two in her eyes. It was a wonderful time for my entire family. We have the performance on tape and still watch it every Christmas.

The boss was always asking me to do numbers that included playing his Lawrence Welk Musical Spoons. They were being sold in toy departments and even music stores across the country. Joe Rizzo, one of the arrangers, and I decided to write a song called "All I Want for Christmas Is a Pair of Spoons." It would be perfect for my children to do on a Christmas show, so I taught them how to play some rhythm patterns, and we put together a routine. I dressed up like Santa Claus in a department store and asked each one what they wanted for Christmas.

"A pair of spoons," they shouted. Unfortunately the dress rehearsal didn't go too well because we had trouble hearing the band. Lawrence decided we should just use a keyboard instrument and he chose a Celeste, positioned right beside the set. It worked, and needless to say, Norma and I gave all the children a pair of Lawrence Welk Spoons for Christmas. However, I don't think I ever heard them play the spoons again after that.

In addition to the marimba and drums, I played a variety of perussion instruments, including spoons, wood blocks, maracas, bells, chimes, coconuts, the triangle—even a kitchen stool.

The kids continued with their lessons. Tim started taking guitar, but the teacher wanted him to sing while he played. It seemed more like a vocal lesson, and Tim was frustrated because he was more interested in the guitar. Terry took up the harmonica for a while, but they all lost interest as they got older. Maybe I should have stepped in and helped them more. Instead of sending them to a teacher, I should have taught them myself, at least the dancing and the drums. But I found myself being a little hard on them at times, and that's why I sent them to someone else for lessons. One thing for sure, they will never forget the times they performed on the Welk Christmas shows.

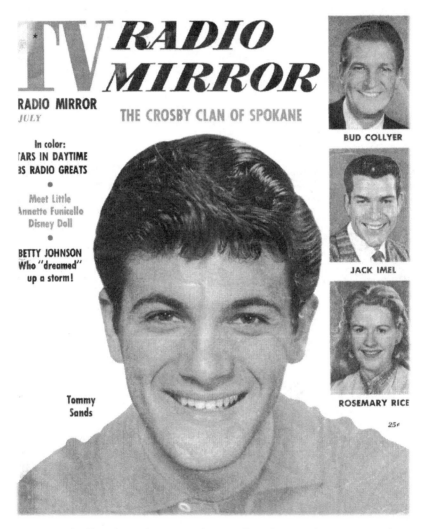

It was a thrill to share the cover of TV Radio Mirror *with Tommy Sands, back in the day when you could buy a magazine for twenty-five cents.*

The magazine article featured a picture of the children gathered around me at the piano with Norma watching on (left to right) Debbie 11, Gregory 13, Timothy 9, Cindy 7, and Terry 5.

TEN

WELK'S BAD BOY

Things were going well for me. I had a wonderful wife, five beautiful kids, a nice home, a secure job, and a new car every year. What more could a person possibly ask for? Well, it seemed that I couldn't stand prosperity. I frequently enjoyed a couple of drinks with the boys after work, but then I started having a few more at home. It was getting out of hand. I began staying out late, and my drinking got worse. I never drank when I worked, but I sure made up for it after the job. It became a real problem at home and reflected in my performance. I was coming home at three or four in the morning, and sometimes I even stayed out all night. There were times when I didn't come home for two or three days. Once when I missed a TV rehearsal, Lawrence called the house, but Norma didn't know where I was.

I was throwing it all away: my family, my job, everything. It was even worse on the road. I stayed out all night and sometimes missed the plane to the next town. On one tour, I missed my flight three days in a row. I would oversleep and not hear the wakeup call. Somehow I always managed to find a flight that would get me there in time for the show, but that's not the way it's supposed to be.

We all had to travel together with the show, and Lawrence always knew if someone missed a flight. He was just about running out of patience with me. After I missed my third consecutive flight, Lawrence decided it was time for me to either change my ways or find another job. When he told me to sit beside him on the plane the next day, I knew I was in trouble.

"Jack," he said, "you've missed the last three flights. Do you have any reason at all why that happened?"

The wheels were turning in my head. I knew I'd better come up with something or he was going to let me go.

"Lawrence, I've always had a hard time waking up in the morning. It's been a problem all my life. I always pack my suitcase and set it by the door. Then I go to bed with my clothes on. That way, if I oversleep, I can jump out of bed, grab my suitcase, and get on the bus to the airport."

Lawrence just looked at me. "You mean to tell me that you go to bed with your clothes on?"

"Yes, sir."

"Jack, you're either a liar or you're crazy or you're on dope. Nobody goes to bed with his clothes on."

Well, he had me, so I finally told him the truth. "I got drunk and didn't hear the wakeup call."

"Why didn't you tell me that in the first place? I don't think I can put up with this kind of behavior much longer."

Lawrence had been given a smoked ham by the Chamber of Commerce in the town we played the night before. He said to me, "We have five days left on this tour. Do you think you could take care of this ham for me until we get back to L.A.? If you can, then maybe I can find a way to salvage your job. Can you do that?"

I breathed a sigh of relief and told him I would guard it with my life—and I did. I took that ham with me everywhere, even to the concerts. It was never out of my sight. When we got back to L.A., I handed it to him, and folks, I was out of the woods.

I started coming straight home after the job and tried to be a better father to my kids, but my stock was still pretty low with Lawrence. I wasn't getting featured as much, and I was afraid I might have trouble keeping my job. I was still drinking some and had gained about twenty-five pounds. Lawrence told me I would have to lose weight or he couldn't put me on camera, especially if I wanted to tap dance. One day he had me step on a scale, and I weighed over two hundred pounds. Lawrence called me into his dressing room and said, "Jack, we're having a guest tap dancer on the show next week. His name is Arthur Duncan, and he can really dance. Maybe you could learn a few new steps from him."

Well, he was right; Art could dance up a storm. His taps were clean, and he was fast as lightning. I was impressed. Art was a guest for two or three shows, and then Lawrence hired him. It didn't take me long to figure out that I'd better change my ways, and fast. I started losing weight and spent more time practicing my dancing. Art was really a nice guy, and we got along well together.

The dance team of Bobby Burgess and Barbara Boylan was one of the most popular acts on the show. Bobby had been with the Mickey Mouse Club as a child. He and Barbara danced mostly ballroom, but Bobby was also quite a tap dancer. Now that I had lost some weight, Lawrence thought maybe the three of us could do a dance together. We worked up a routine to the song "Buck Dance," a tune Woody Herman had recorded in the 1940s that was perfect for a tap dance. We performed it on the TV show, and Lawrence asked us to come up with some more routines. My job situation was starting to look better, but I still wasn't being featured much tap dancing while playing the marimba. During my first four or five years with the show, I had been performing almost every week.

Lawrence hired a great Dixieland jazz trombone player named Bob Havens who also played the vibraphone. A vibraphone has metal bars and a pedal to sustain the notes, while the marimba has wooden bars, so you have to roll the mallets to get the same effect. Bob and I worked up a routine to "Tiger Rag" where we both played on the vibes and alternated choruses, with Bob on the trombone and me tap dancing. It turned out really well, so Lawrence told us to come up with some more routines. I was now being teamed up with Bob Havens and tap dancing with Art and Bobby. At least I was getting on camera and playing some parts with the band.

Lawrence was still in doubt about my behavior, but I'd had a change of attitude and now walked the straight and narrow.

Sometimes I would suggest a production idea to our producer and director, Jim Hobson, that involved certain people and songs. Welk had so much talent in his cast that I felt we could do more things to include the whole group. Jim liked most of my ideas and even used some of them occasionally. One night Jim did a production number that caught Lawrence's attention, and after the show he commented on how much he liked it.

"I can't really take all the credit," Jim told him. "Most of those ideas came from Ace."

"Jack Imel?" Lawrence asked. "You mean they were his ideas? Are you kidding me? Well, maybe we should have Jack come to one of our production meetings and see what else he has to offer."

I was told to come to the next meeting, and I must have spent the entire night writing down ideas and songs I thought Lawrence might like. I went to the meeting dressed in a shirt and tie. I even carried a small briefcase with all my ideas in it. Lawrence seemed impressed.

After the meeting, Jim told me I did a good job, and I was asked back for the next production meeting. I started writing down ideas and grouping them in categories. We had a theme each week to base the music on. For instance, if the theme was the railroad, we did train songs. Or, we might feature Cole Porter and perform songs he'd written.

After I'd been attending the meetings for almost a year, both Lawrence and Jim agreed that I had contributed enough to become part of the production staff; I was promoted to assistant producer. That meant that I was listed in the credits and would now receive a regular salary. I also produced the road shows, including the three weeks we did every year at Harrah's Club in Lake Tahoe.

This was special. In the past, our road shows had not included group numbers, and there was no lineup. All the singers sat on the side of the stage in chairs, and Lawrence would choose the performers as we went along. No one knew who would be next. Our streamlined wardrobe consisted only of red blazers for the band and male singers, one set of dresses for the Lennon Sisters, and a gown for Alice Lon.

Actually, having Lawrence pick from random went pretty well because he knew how to work an audience and how to pace the show. It gave the sound people a lot of problems, however, because they never knew which mic would be needed next, and Lois Lamont had to guess which lights to use. The show opened and closed with the band; there were no group numbers. Jim and I talked to Lawrence about how the show was being presented, and he agreed that it might be good to include a few group numbers with costumes. But make no mistake, even with those changes, it was Lawrence who pieced the show together. No doubt about it, Welk was the star of his own show. He knew what his audience liked, and he had the talent to make it happen.

I was featured in a group number, "Powder your Face with Sunshine," and everyone was pulling for me.

ELEVEN

THE SIXTIES

The show saw a lot of changes in the sixties, not only broadcasting in color, but personnel turnover as well. Big Tiny Little, a great ragtime and jazz piano player, formed a band and went out on his own, entertaining mostly in casinos throughout Nevada. He was replaced by the multitalented and popular Jo Ann Castle. She played a hot ragtime piano and could hold her own with the best of them on the accordion. She also danced and sang. Jo Ann was a terrific help to me when we did production numbers together, and I always looked forward to performing with her.

The Lennon Sisters also decided to leave us in the 1960s. They had their own TV show with Jimmy Durante and later worked with headliners in Las Vegas and top venues all over the country. They were a big part of our show, and I was sorry to see them go. With four girls gone, it left Lawrence short on personnel, especially in production. But he always kept his eyes open for talent, and it wasn't long before we discovered some great new personalities.

One of the first acts to come along was Sandi Griffiths and Sally Flynn, a singing duet from Utah. They were beautiful girls with voices to match. Then Lawrence found Gail Farrell—Miss

Oklahoma. She had a terrific voice, could play the piano, and was an outstanding vocal arranger. They all looked great on camera.

When Champagne Lady Alice Lon departed in 1959, we decided to bring in a female guest each week until we found a successor. That went on for a year until Norma Zimmer came along. She was beautiful in every way: voice and looks, with a personality as sweet as they come. Lawrence hired her after her first appearance. Her resume boasted a long list of credits that included singing backup for Frank Sinatra, Perry Como, and as the voice of the White Rose in Disney's *Alice in Wonderland*. The audience loved her and we did too. What a nice lady. She stayed with the Welk Family for twenty-two years until the run ended in 1982.

As the show welcomed new faces during the 1960s, we really hit the jackpot. There was a restaurant across the street from Lawrence's office called The Horn where performers would gather and sing songs. Rick, the owner, had been a vocal coach for some of the studios in Hollywood. Everyone who came in and sang was a professional, so it was always entertaining to spend an evening at The Horn.

Curt Ramsey on our staff stopped in one night to hear the music. The next day he came to the production meeting and raved about a girl singer he'd heard there, Ralna English, and told us we should invite her to one of our rehearsals. When she showed up, we were all knocked out, and Lawrence hired her right there on the spot. She sang jazz, big band, religious, and country music—she could do it all. Favorable mail started pouring in, and we knew we had a winner.

Ralna said she and her husband, Guy Hovis, would like to sing a duet for our next Christmas show. Believe me, when we heard them sing together, there was consensus that we would now have a marvelous married couple performing on the show. A year later, they had become one of our most popular acts, and it stayed that way right up until the final taping.

Lawrence had a sixth sense about recognizing talent, and he sure found it in Mary Lou Metzger. She could sing and dance and really had a feel for show business. Lawrence met her after one of our tapings and asked her to sing for him; he hired her without hesitation. She looked like a million dollars on camera.

We put her in a production number one night, and all she had to do was skip across the stage dressed like a little girl. She moved like a dancer, so I asked if she had ever studied dance. She said she started dancing when she was young and had been cast in the road show version of *The Music Man*. That was good enough for me. We worked up a routine and showed it to the boss. He liked it, and from then on we were often paired together. We found success with numbers that told a story like a skit. We chose the songs, and Rose Weiss found the right costumes. Mary Lou and I would work up a tap dance, throw in a little dialogue, and we were off and running. I think it had been a while since she had tap danced, but she was a fast study and lit up like a Christmas tree on camera.

Working with Mary Lou Metzger was always fun.

Being assistant producer made it difficult for me to perform sometimes. I had to create production ideas, help put the show together, stage the group numbers, and organize the road show. My marimba playing suffered the most. You can't leave this instrument for long periods of time and still keep your technique. But working with Mary Lou was fun, and it showed on camera.

Mary Lou graduated from Temple University with a degree in theater arts, and this made our collaborations very smooth. We never had an argument over anything during all those years. A lot of the ideas we used were hers. We still see each other once a year when she holds an open house in January. It's sort of a New Year's gathering, and everyone from the Welk Show is invited. Norma and I really look forward to it.

Mary Lou's career in show business kept getting better year after year. She hosted for the Welk TV shows seen on PBS and even produced and directed them when some of us went on the road as a group. She also produced the Welk Christmas specials we did in Escondido, California, and at the Champagne Theatre in Branson (Welk Resort).

During the 1960s, Jo Ann Castle left the show to go out on her own. She has done very well, earning a standing ovation every time she performed. She's a great entertainer and one of the most popular performers Welk ever had.

Myron Floren probably had the most work away from the show. He was Welk's right-hand man and in charge of everything on the road. Whenever the band had time off, Myron was always booked somewhere else, and like Jo Ann, he always received a standing ovation. He could do an entire two-hour concert by himself. He practiced constantly, and it showed. Myron was easy to work with and hardly ever raised his voice. Like Mary Lou said one time, "He was the heart of the Lawrence Welk band."

Other people Lawrence hired during the sixties were Andra Willis, Natalie Nevins, and Tanya Falan. Tanya really had a tough audition. She came to a production meeting, and Lawrence had her sit in a chair and sing with no accompaniment in front of six guys. We were all impressed by this beautiful girl with the great voice. Tanya later became Welk's daughter-in-law when she married his son Larry.

We had a male quartet called The Blenders. Barbara Boylan, Bobby Burgess' dance partner, fell in love with Greg Dixon of this group. They got married and moved on to raise a family. This left Bobby without a partner, so he did the same thing Lawrence had done in looking for a Champagne Lady. He brought in a different dance partner every week until he found the right one. After a few weeks of auditions, Cissy King from Albuquerque took her turn. She was a fine and versatile dancer, having studied ballet, acrobatics, ballroom, and tap. Cissy also sang and had a sparkling personality.

Every year we did a show featuring songs made popular by country singers. This always brought a good reaction from the audience, so Lawrence started looking for a country singer. He discovered Lynn Anderson, who could really sing a country song. The camera loved her, but she didn't stay with the show very long. I think she felt more comfortable working with country musicians. Lynn left for Nashville where she recorded "Rose Garden," which went to number one on the country charts and earned her an award. I know she always felt grateful to Lawrence for giving her career a start.

During this time, Lawrence became chairman of the Cancer Society, which meant traveling to different cities, giving talks, and raising money for cancer research. At one of those fundraising banquets, he met country singer Clay Hart. Lawrence invited him to appear on the show, and Clay made such a big impression that he was hired. You would always find him in some corner practicing his guitar and singing. He was a remarkable songwriter too.

Speaking of guitar, Buddy Merrill had to leave the show to go into the Army. Lawrence told him his job would be waiting for him when he got out of the military. While Buddy was serving his country, Lawrence hired Neil LeVang. Neil was unbelievable on string instruments and played banjo, mandolin, and violin. He'd had a local television show in Seattle called *Fiddlin' Neil*. When Buddy was discharged, Lawrence didn't want to let Neil go, so he decided to keep them both. When Clay joined Buddy and Neil, we had a real country sound whenever we needed it.

Other changes came when Lawrence hired alto player Dave Edwards and bassist Richard Maloof, who also played the tuba, which added some oompah-pah depth to our marches and polkas.

We enlarged the string section by hiring Charlotte Harris on the cello, the only female in the Welk orchestra. She was a studied musician and provided such a full sound. Charlotte was featured quite often playing a solo and always received good mail.

Our audience liked to hear the band play a waltz or a ballad, and Jerry Burke on the organ was a favorite. Jerry passed away in the early 1960s and was missed by everyone. Lawrence had played his family's pump organ back on the farm when he was growing up and loved the sound. His search for a new organist found Bob Ralston, who also played classical piano and was an arranger. He had been with the Freddie Martin Orchestra and fit right in with the Champagne Music style. In all the years I worked with Bob, I can honestly say that I don't ever remember him making a mistake. His technique was remarkable.

Lawrence also hired Bob Smale, a great piano player, marvelous arranger, and one of the nicest guys you will ever meet. Our rhythm section was bigger than most other bands and featured two pianos, an organ, bass, three guitars, accordion, drums, and myself on mallets, for a total of ten in just that one section. Then we also had four in the violin section, five reeds, four trombones, and four trumpets for a grand total of twenty-seven pieces. What a great sound, especially on instrumentals. It was the best band I'd ever heard—and what an honor to be a part of it.

Animal trainer Mary Lou Metzger reveals that it's actually me in the bear costume. Oh surprise!

When we began broadcasting in color, it gave the show an entirely new look. Viewers could now see the beautiful sets designed by our art director, Chuck Coons. It also showcased our wonderful wardrobe lady, Rose Weiss, who did an amazing job of selecting colors and styles. Rose had excellent taste in designing the clothes we wore, getting them to fit just right. The band had at least four colored blazers and several different suits in the latest styles. If anyone was unhappy about wearing a certain garment, she would do her best to change it; but that seldom happened, as she was on the money most of the time.

Rose had a knack for dressing us as characters in production numbers. Those outfits were rented at Western Costumes in Hollywood. They carried anything you could possibly need, from Frankenstein to a robot. Being dressed like an animal seemed to be my specialty. Over the years, I performed as an ape, a bear, an elephant, a bull, a penguin—you name it.

I remember one particular number called "If I Could Talk to the Animals" when we played the Indiana State Fair where it was a sweltering hundred degrees on the stage. I wore an ape costume, and Larry Hooper was dressed like Dr. Doolittle. At the end of the act, I had to walk out, throw my arms around him and say, "I really go ape for you, Doc."

There I am beating the drums in a number called "Down in Jungle Town" wearing the infamous ape suit.

My ape suit looked like the real thing and had been used in a couple of Tarzan movies. But, man, was it ever hot inside, like being in a sauna. This was a ten-day tour, and by the fifth day, Larry asked me to wait until the very last second to come out and put my arms around him. He said, "Ace, I can't get that last note out."

The suit was starting to get real gamey, so I poured a whole bottle of Aqua Velva Ice Blue Cooling Aftershave in it, but that only made it worse. By the end of that tour, my monkey suit smelled like a real-life ape. When I returned it to ABC Studios, the wardrobe department refused to take it out of the box at first, but they finally worked up enough courage. Needless to say, we never did that number again on the road.

Ken Delo was another talented addition to the Welk Show during the sixties. Not only could he sing, but he also did comedy. He wrote some songs, and even published a children's book called *The Ugly Christmas Tree*. For several years, he had his own TV show in Australia, one of the highest rated shows in that country. When Larry Welk opened the Champagne Theatre in Branson, Ken performed there and emceed the show. We worked together for several seasons in Branson. Ken's wife, Marilyn, became good friends with Norma, and we still get together once in a while. Ken and Marilyn now live in Gilbert, Arizona, and he is still performing.

Lawrence had a lot of behind-the-scene heroes. There was Ralph Portner with his great sense of humor. He was the announcer for our radio show, which aired every weekend from the Aragon Ballroom, and later from the Hollywood Palladium. He also wrote some songs with Joe Rizzo that we played on the TV show. Versatile Joe arranged all our Latin numbers, along with big band instrumentals and vocals.

George "Gus" Thow, a Harvard graduate, played trumpet for years with the Welk band, and before that, he was with the Dorsey Brothers Orchestra. He also played on soundtracks for several motion pictures. Gus later retired his trumpet to write all of the introductions for *The Lawrence Welk Show*. It wasn't easy writing for Lawrence because, with his heavy German accent, there were a lot of words he had trouble pronouncing. It was tricky, but somehow Gus always managed to get the job done.

Lois Lamont, Lawrence's secretary, handled all of his business correspondence. She started out with Lawrence way back when he still had a polka band known as The Hotsy Totsy

Boys. Believe it or not, she also worked the lights when we went on the road.

It seems like all of Lawrence's people could do more than one thing. Several girls handled the fan mail, including Margaret Huron. When Lois eventually retired, Margaret took her place. Anything you wanted to find out about, she had the answers. Much of the success the Welk Show is still having on PBS is due to Margaret.

The top man behind the scenes was, of course, our producer and director, Jim Hobson. He was responsible for everything you saw when you watched *The Lawrence Welk Show*. He had been a cameraman and director for *The Liberace Show*, which was a huge success in the 1950s. I can honestly say that I never heard Jim lose his temper with anyone, and he was always open to suggestions. If you were unhappy about something, he could straighten it out. Jim had a lively imagination and super knowledge about cameras. If anybody wondered what Lawrence liked or disliked, Jim Hobson could figure it out most of the time. He never questioned any of Welk's suggestions or ideas. Jim devoted his life to making the Welk Show entertaining and successful. I can't say enough about Jim. All of the crew and technicians respected him, and that went for the band, the singers, and dancers as well.

In the mid-1960s, we received some unexpected bad news. The Dodge Corporation decided they could no longer sponsor the show. They had been wonderful and treated us with so much respect that we had no clue this was going to happen. We all had to turn in our Dodge cars, of course, but they offered us great prices if we wanted to buy the car we were driving. Most of us did. The big Dodge sign draped behind the band on stage had to go, but even through all of these changes, Lawrence maintained a good relationship with the Chrysler people.

Finding another sponsor was not much of a problem because the Welk Show was still very popular and had good ratings. By the time we were ready to start the fall season, we had our new sponsor: J. B. Williams & Company. They sold Geritol, Poligrip, Sominex, Aqua Velva, and Serutan ("that's Nature's spelled backwards"), just to mention a few. These were the kind of products our audience would buy. We changed out the Dodge sign with an even bigger one for Geritol. We sometimes made joking remarks on TV about some of the products, but always being careful not to offend J. B. Williams.

Gus Thow, who wrote all of Welk's announcements, was very clever about that and—oh yes—we received all of these products free of charge. Some of us were approaching the age when these items came in handy, especially the Geritol and Serutan. Even though we weren't sponsored by Dodge anymore, Lawrence personally bought me a new Dodge every two or three years as a bonus for being on the production staff.

TWELVE

BOMB THREATS AND BUFFALO HERDS

I have mentioned the drinking problems I had after I joined the show, but being on the production staff presented a new kind of challenge for me. Lawrence didn't approve of everything I suggested for the show. I was always looking for different songs, especially humorous ones. He liked most of my ideas, but once in a while I would come into the meeting with something he didn't understand at all. That happened with "You Can't Roller Skate in a Buffalo Herd," a song that featured a play on words written by Roger Miller.

Welk was out of town for the Cancer Foundation and wasn't present at the meeting when I suggested it. Jim Hobson and the staff liked the song and the way I wanted to stage it. The lyrics went something like this: "You can't roller skate in a buffalo herd, unless you have a mind to. You can't go fishing in a watermelon patch, unless you have a mind to. You can't go swimming in a baseball pool, unless you have a mind to."

The song went on and on like that, and I thought it was very clever. My idea was to stage it in a saloon during the Wild West days. I would stroll in as an old-time philosopher and start singing this song. Well, when we rehearsed the number on the day of the show, someone brought the lyrics to Lawrence's attention and told him the song didn't make any sense. We had spent quite a bit of money on the set and a lot of time rehearsing it. Jim talked Lawrence into keeping the song in the show because it was a big hit on the country charts, but I knew Lawrence didn't get the humor, and I was going to hear about it. I walked into the production meeting the next day, and Lawrence was waiting for me. He was sitting at his desk, wearing his glasses, and reading the sheet music.

"Before we start the meeting," he said, "I want to talk about some of the songs we've been doing, especially the ones Jack Imel has suggested. I would like to read these lyrics to you. 'You can't roller skate in a buffalo herd. You can't roller skate in a buffalo herd. You can't roller skate in a buffalo herd, unless you have a mind to.'"

He took off his glasses and looked all around. "Everybody knows you can't roller skate in a buffalo herd. Let me continue." He put his glasses back on.

"'You can't go fishing in a watermelon patch. You can't go fishing in a watermelon patch. You can't go fishing in a watermelon patch, unless you have a mind to.'"

He took off his glasses again and said, "This song doesn't make any sense. Nobody goes fishing in a watermelon patch."

He put his glasses back on and read, "'You can't go swimming in a baseball pool.' Need I go any further? This song just doesn't make any sense. How can you go swimming in a baseball pool?"

Lawrence didn't see the humor, and no one came to my aid. "We're going to have to watch Jack's judgment on his taste in songs. He has a habit of going off on the deep end."

Needless to say, the only songs I suggested for the next couple of months were "God Bless America" and "The Lord's Prayer." But who can say he was wrong? Maybe his audience didn't think it made any sense either. We came up with a new slogan on the production staff: "If Lawrence don't understand it, the audience won't understand it." Lawrence thought I used bad judgment at times, and there would be no more of it.

Coming up with new and different ideas every week was a challenge, but I got an idea for a production that I thought could be great for our run at Harrah's. Lawrence had just released an album of songs from *No, No, Nanette*. I went to him and presented my idea of doing a medley of songs we had recorded from the musical using the entire cast to close the show.

"Sounds good," he said.

I explained that we'd close the medley with the dancers dancing to "I Want to Be Happy," but instead of using just the five of us (Art, Bobby, Cissy, Mary Lou, and myself), we would use eighteen dancers.

"Eighteen? But that's impossible. We don't have that many dancers."

"I'll teach them," I explained. "I know some steps that would be easy to learn, and if they do them together as a group, it could be very effective."

"But how long will it take you to teach them?" he asked.

"Only a couple of months."

"You're kidding."

"Just give me a couple of weeks," I said, "and if it doesn't look possible, I'll forget it."

"It sounds like a good idea, but I can't see some of my people tap dancing. You'll have to prove it to me."

"That's okay with me."

I sure hoped I was right. Two weeks wasn't much time, but I could get help from Mary Lou and the rest of the dancers. Kenny Trimble, a trombone player, protested "You're not going to put tap shoes on me, Ace. I'm a musician."

Well, after the first couple of rehearsals, Kenny said "Man, I dig this. It's a lot of fun." Even Joe Feeney, the Irish tenor, started to show promise. The gang really worked hard. We crammed about six or seven rehearsals into the two weeks. Then we had to buy thirteen pairs of tap shoes. This idea of mine was starting to look expensive. All I could think about was that it better work out. After a couple of weeks, I asked Lawrence to give me just one more week. Then it was time to show the boss.

They were a little ragged, but good enough that Lawrence felt it would work. We still had some time, so we kept rehearsing, and each time we could see improvement. When we opened at Harrah's, it was really looking good. After we got the costumes from Rose Weiss and added the lighting, the number looked terrific. We did it on television the following year, and I must say,

I was proud of the number and the fun we had putting it together.

I taught the entire cast of Music Makers how to tap dance to "I Want to Be Happy" for the grand finale of our Harrah's engagement.

One night we were playing to a sold-out crowd in a new building that held close to 18,000 people in Landover, Maryland. The first half of the show had gone smoothly. About ten minutes into the second half, I was approached by a man in uniform—the fire marshal. He asked if I was the producer.

"Yes."

"Well, we got a problem," he said. "We just had a phone call from a man who claims a bomb's going off in fifteen minutes. He's going to call back in five minutes. We get a lot of calls like this, so let's see what he has to say when he calls back. It's all up to you. We can get the members of the show out of the building, but it would cause a major panic if we tell the audience. I'll get back to you the minute he calls."

Well, it was something for sure; I was about to panic. I tried to locate Lon Varnell, the promoter, but he was nowhere to be found. All I could do was to wait for the fire marshal to come backstage. My heart was beating like a drum. This was the longest five minutes I could ever remember.

He finally returned and said, "We just received a second phone call from this guy. He claims we got ten minutes. Like I told you, we get calls like this all the time, but there's something about him that makes us think he might be on the level."

Without hesitation I said, "We gotta get Lawrence and everyone in the show out of this place." I went on stage and quietly told Lawrence and the band members to slowly walk off the stage and out of the building to the far end of the parking lot.

"Jack, why are we doing this?" Welk wanted to know.

"Because there's a bomb going off in about ten minutes," I answered.

The fire marshal ushered us out the back door and into the parking lot. The audience had no idea what was going on, but they knew something was wrong.

Now here's the picture. The entire cast huddled at the end of the parking lot waiting to see if a building holding 18,000 people was going to blow up. Well, the ten minutes went by and nothing happened. I'll be honest with you. I knew if nothing happened, I was in real trouble with the boss. It's awful to say, but I almost hoped something would happen just to save my job. About fifteen minutes later, we went back on stage and finished the show. I thought my job was finished as well. After the show, Welk asked me why I didn't tell him first.

"The entire show is my responsibility," I replied. "What if a bomb did go off? That would be the end of *The Lawrence Welk Show*. I'd be the only survivor. How could I live with that?"

He was pretty nice about it, but he told me if this ever happened again to tell him first. I felt relieved. Lawrence made some excuse to the audience; we finished the show that day, and went on with the tour. Fortunately, we never had another bomb scare after that.

THIRTEEN

THE SHOW GOES LIVE

We still did around twenty one-nighters a year. Lawrence loved going on the road and performing in front of thousands of people because he wasn't as relaxed on television. Every word he said was printed out for him. He wouldn't say so much as "Good evening, friends," unless it was on a cue card.

When the show went live with ABC, even cue cards weren't always the answer. I'll never forget the night we did a show where the theme was music from World War I. The cue-card boy had written World War I with the numeral "1." Lawrence came out that night and said, "Tonight all the songs you're going to hear are from World War Eye." Instead of saying *one*, he pronounced it as the letter *"I."* But his audience was used to hearing him say things like that and loved him for it. He was a master showman, but without cue cards on the road, he would often say things that made you wonder: *Did he really say that?*

One time we were playing in Evansville, Indiana, the hometown of Alvin Ashby, one of our singers, so this was his big night. This is how Lawrence introduced him: "Now here's the one you've been waiting for, Alvin Ashby from Evansville, Indiana. Come out here, Alvin, and tell the folks your name and where you're from."

Well, I guess he said he was Alvin Ashby from Evansville, Indiana, but the one that takes the blue ribbon happened in Pittsburgh, Pennsylvania. We were playing for the Shriner's Convention with close to 10,000 people in the audience. Now I would always check with the boss in his dressing room about thirty minutes before a concert, in case we had any problems with sound or stage setups. I was in his dressing room when someone knocked on the door, so I answered it. It was the gentleman in charge of entertainment for the Shriners, and he wanted to say hello to Lawrence. Of course, I let him in and introduced him to the boss.

"I know you have your show plan for tonight," he said to Lawrence, "but I was wondering if you'd be so kind as to introduce the Grand Potentate and his wife who are sitting in the front row. Maybe you could do that just before you start your show."

Welk had that puzzled look on his face, and I knew we were in trouble. He couldn't pronounce potentate, let alone know what it meant.

"Lawrence," I said, "the Grand Potentate is like the Exalted Ruler of the Elks." Lawrence could relate to that because he belonged to the Elks Lodge.

"Oh, well then, we'd better introduce him."

When the man left, Welk looked at me and asked, "How do you pronounce that word?"

"Potentate."

He must have asked me at least four or five times. Okay, so then it was showtime, and Lawrence was ready to walk on stage. He turned to me one more time and asked, "Now how do you pronounce that word?"

"Potentate," I repeated, "potentate."

Lawrence walked to the center mic. "Before we start our show tonight, I would like to introduce sitting in the front row, the Grand Totem Pole and his wife."

Well, for a moment there was dead silence. Then people started to laugh, and within seconds, the place went up in smoke. After that, Lawrence couldn't do anything wrong the rest of the night. Needless to say, the band was in tears.

One year Lawrence wanted to open the show dressed up like a beatnik, along with our guitar players—you know, long hair, sparkly shirts, and headbands. The band started by playing the usual Champagne Music. Then beatnik Lawrence walked out and stopped the music. When the guitars came out behind him, we all started playing rock and roll. It was a fun idea, but we had to hide Welk backstage so no one would see how he was dressed until it was time.

In one venue, the backstage area was just a few feet from the back door, so we took him outside. No one realized that the door would automatically lock when it was closed, and Lawrence couldn't get back in. It was time to start the show, and Welk was pounding on the door. A security guard opened the door, but wouldn't let him in. When Welk finally took off his wig, the guard apologized, and the show went on as scheduled.

Bobby and Cissy used to do the polka and then invite audience participation. A few of the women would dance with Bobby, and some of the men danced with Cissy. Then Lawrence decided it would be fun to plant a girl and boy in the audience. They were really good polka dancers from Los Angeles, and they traveled with us. One night Bobby was dancing with the girl when her wig accidentally flew off. Well, that brought the house down. Embarrassed, the girl dove under the piano and hid. It got more reaction than anything we'd ever done, so Lawrence said to leave it in. The girl really knew how to play it up, and she stopped the show every night. The audience never caught on that they were actually part of the performance.

Joe Feeney had to come on next, and if anyone could follow that act it was Joe, because everyone loved his voice. Of course, we couldn't use that wig bit if we played the same town again. We tried doing it on television once, but it didn't get the same reaction as on the road. I think a lot of people figured that if it really was an accident, we would have stopped the tape.

We were in for a shock in 1971 when ABC decided they no longer wanted to carry the Welk Show on their network. None of us had any idea this was going to happen, and that went for Lawrence too. He found out while playing golf when a news reporter ran out onto the course and asked him if he had any comment about *The Lawrence Welk Show* being canceled.

"It's news to me," Lawrence answered.

I guess nothing is really sacred in show business, but Lawrence wasn't about to give up television without a fight. His good friend Don Fedderson, who produced *The Liberace Show*, *My Three Sons*, *Family Affair*, and *Petticoat Junction*, just to name a few, came to our rescue. Don said the show was too popular to be taken off the air. ABC claimed our ratings were down, and they were looking for shows that appealed to a younger audience.

Don Fedderson contacted every television station in the country and told them that the Welk Show was available. Within a few weeks, we had positive answers from over two hundred stations. This was the start of a long and lasting career in syndication. Our paychecks never stopped when we switched from network to syndication. To be truthful, I didn't worry when ABC canceled us. That's how much confidence I had in the Welk organization. However, ABC should at least have had the courtesy to tell Lawrence personally what was happening, instead of letting him be humiliated on the golf course. After all, the Welk Show had contributed a great deal to the success of that network.

When I joined Welk back in 1957, the show was produced at Studio E, which was the only one on the lot, and it had a long history. That's where they filmed the first talkie, *The Jazz Singer*, starring Al Jolson. There were no dressing rooms, so we used trailers: one for the men, one for the girls, and one for Welk. By the early 1960s, ABC had to build more studios for their new shows, and the size of the lot became enormous—all because of *The Lawrence Welk Show*. However, we knew it was best for us to continue taping the syndicated show at Studio E. We had been there for almost fifteen years, and the crew knew exactly what our producer, Jim Hobson, wanted. J. B. Williams was still our sponsor, so nothing really changed that much.

FOURTEEN

TURN OFF THE BUBBLE MACHINE

We played several large venues that were built in the sixties and seventies. Rupp Arena in Lexington, Kentucky, held well over 20,000 people, and we sold out. The most famous one was the new Madison Square Garden. We filled it on a Sunday afternoon, and this was during the years when crime was at its peak. Welk had been told he wasn't that popular in the New York City area. Well, he proved them wrong.

The Superdome in New Orleans holds 72,000 people, so we didn't fill that, of course, but we still had a big turnout. We also performed in some of the older venues such as Boston Garden. With seats on the playing floor, it could hold close to 20,000 people. It was summertime, and there was no air conditioning; the temperature on stage reached over one hundred degrees. Welk actually let the band members take off their jackets for that one. The dressing rooms were dirty, and most of the clothes racks were broken. Four paramedic vehicles were needed during the concert. It was a terrible experience, and Welk refused to play there ever again.

Our biggest stage was outdoors in Toronto, and it covered half a football field. The Canadian audiences were great, and some of the Welk people still perform there from time to time.

Other venues included the World's Fair in Seattle where the Space Needle had just been built.

Minnesota had the largest state fair in the country, but that presented some unusual challenges I had never experienced before. Like most fairs, there was a racetrack between the grandstand and the stage. Usually they place folding chairs on the racetrack before the show begins, but not here. Half of the stage was under the grandstand and had to be pulled out with a cable. Then they attached it to the rest of the stage on the infield. This meant we couldn't set up the mics for the performers, although we could put our bandstand on the infield portion of the stage.

Another complication involved a thrill show on the racetrack that took place right before our show. We were to start after them, and the stage under the grandstand would be pulled out while we were doing the opening number with our entire cast of singers. There was no way to get everyone on stage, and an even bigger challenge was getting Welk on stage. That was nearly impossible, to say the least.

I went to the manager of the fair and told him my problem, with no success. How was I going to explain this to Welk? I had learned my lesson with the bomb scare in Maryland, so I called the agent who had booked us there, Frank Taylor. Unfortunately, he wasn't in his hotel room, and again, this was long before cell phones. I left a message at the hotel, but Frank never returned my call. I would have to explain this to Lawrence when he arrived at the fairgrounds, which was about an hour before the show time.

When he arrived, I tried to describe how the stage was built in two parts and would come together during the opening number. He looked at me like I had lost my mind, and I couldn't blame him. It didn't make any sense to me either.

"Jack, have you been drinking?"

"No."

"Get me Frank Taylor," he said.

By then Frank was just outside Welk's dressing room. I explained the problem to him, but he said we'd just have to go along with them. With only fifteen minutes left before our show, I looked out and noticed the two parts of the stage had already been put together. The manager I talked to earlier had changed his mind. He told the thrill show people to shorten their act so they would have time to set the stage for the Welk Show.

I was so exasperated that I was ready to tell Lawrence he should find someone else for the job. I guess Lawrence talked to the manager after the show, and he explained everything. Lawrence shook my hand and said, "Nice job." All I can say is, I was glad to get back home. Even though I loved my job, I wasn't sure if I really wanted to be a producer. It was just too much to be a producer and then perform too.

One of Welk's most popular trademarks was the bubble machine. He could also make a sound with his finger in his mouth that resembled a champagne bottle being uncorked. It was very important that we set up the two bubble machines on the road shows, with one on each side of the stage. They usually sat on top of a speaker, and we had to be careful that the bubbles didn't land on the stage. The liquid solution that formed the bubbles was soapy and made the stage slippery, almost like ice.

We learned our lesson the first year we played at Harrah's. On TV we placed the machines behind the bandstand with electric fans to keep the bubbles from drifting onto the stage. But at Harrah's, the fans didn't help because a draft made the bubbles scatter downstage. So we decided to place the machines on each side of the stage with the curtain closed. Well, that would have worked fine, except the stage was already saturated with the bubble solution; it looked like glass.

Welk took about three steps on his entrance and fell backwards, landing on his back. I hurried out to help him and fell flat on my back too. Neither of us could get on our feet. Jock Vogt, Harrah's stage manager, closed the curtains, and some of the crew helped us off. What a way to start the show. It took about fifteen minutes to clean up the stage. Lawrence explained to the audience what had happened, and then we went on with the show. It was a miracle that Lawrence didn't seriously hurt himself. From that day on, we were very careful where we set up those bubble machines. Welk never blamed me for the incident. It seems like our road shows always had an adventure of some sort.

FIFTEEN

THE SEVENTIES

The 1970s brought about some more changes. One day I was setting up the show in St. Paul, Minnesota, when a good-looking man came up and asked me what time Mr. Welk would be arriving. He was Tom Netherton and said he was supposed to be on the show that night. Welk usually told me when we were going to have a guest on, but I guess it must have slipped his mind.

When Welk arrived, I introduced them to each other. Tom had been recommended by a close friend of Lawrence's, so he and Bob Smale, our piano player, worked out a song together. That night Tom sang "If Ever I Should Leave You," and the audience loved it. Lawrence invited him to come to Los Angeles to make a guest appearance on the TV show, and a couple of weeks later Tom was hired. Our audience, especially the women, loved him, and the mail started pouring in. He had the right chemistry. Within a year, he was one of our most popular performers. Welk had him sing to the ladies in the audience, and they adored him.

During this time, some of our singers decided to leave the show: Natalie Nevins, Andra Willis, Sally Flynn, Lynn Anderson, Clay Hart, and our cello player, Charlotte Harris. Clay and Sally fell in love and were married. When they performed together, she would play "Orange Blossom Special" on the violin, and it brought the house down. Vocally they sounded great, and Clay's guitar playing was outstanding.

Some new faces joined the show when Lawrence hired country singer Ava Barber and her husband, Roger Sullivan, who played drums. Roger played behind Ava and was also featured with Johnny Klein and me doing Glenn Miller's famous "St. Louis Blues March."

John Klein decided to retire in the early 1970s. Besides being the drummer, he drove the truck that carried all the band instruments and equipment and helped Barney Liddell and me set up the bandstand. The stage crew I had in each town we played was helpful, but if I needed something done fast, Barney and John were the answer.

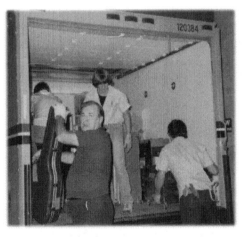

Barney Liddell could always be counted on to set up the bandstand at each tour stop.

When John left the band, we were without a drummer, so I filled in. I knew most of the Welk charts because I had been the drummer for nine weeks on the road—and that was in addition to being the assistant producer, staging production numbers, and performing with Mary Lou. Finally, we hired Paul Humphrey, one of the top studio drummers in Los Angeles, and he recorded several of the Welk albums. Paul had played with a lot of big bands and was perfect for the job.

But this still left us without someone to help me set up when we were on the road. Ava Barber's husband, Roger, told me he'd like to help, and that sounded like a good idea. I suggested him to Welk and got the okay. Roger did a fabulous job, and we used a lot of his suggestions. He learned fast and was a hard worker.

Ava recorded a song called "Bucket to the South" that made it to the country charts in Billboard. She could sing any kind of song we asked her to, but her specialty was always country. She also had a great sense of humor.

While giving talks for the Cancer Society, Lawrence discovered the five Semonski Sisters from Pennsylvania. We put them on the TV show and hired them after a few appearances. He also found the two Aldridge Sisters and the identical Otwell Twins, all great additions to the show. We eventually teamed them up together to sing country songs and some of the popular tunes of the day.

The last few years of the road show, Lawrence decided to have a Champagne Lady in every town we performed in. It wasn't necessary to sing, they only had to write in a hundred words or less why they watched *The Lawrence Welk Show*. The winner in each town would read her letter, and sometimes they sang, but none of them really made an impression on Welk until we played Madison, Wisconsin.

I introduced the winner, Kathie Sullivan, to Lawrence before the show, and he invited her to sing a few bars. Lawrence stopped her after only eight bars of "The Sound of Music."

"That's the most beautiful voice I ever heard." Lawrence hired her right there in his dressing room. Kathie did have a beautiful voice and a nice personality; most of her songs were from musical comedies.

Jim Turner was the last singer Lawrence hired. Jim favored country music, but he could sing any kind of song. He also played the guitar, and in fact, he performed at my son Tim's wedding.

Having so many singers meant teaming some of them together because it became difficult to feature each one every week. We kept getting letters from our fans saying they wanted to hear the band more, and Lawrence was quoted once as saying, "The band is the star of the show."

Welk was still packing them in doing one-nighters. He had one of the best promoters in the business with Lon Varnell. Lon promoted some big stars, and he told me that none of them sold out like Welk. That was Welk's history, even back in the thirties and forties when they booked ballrooms. The famous bandleader Paul Whiteman once said, "I never wanted to play a city where Lawrence Welk had just played. Nobody could follow that."

We performed for three days at the Montana State Fair in Billings. After the first show, a lot of Welk people went out to a country music bar that featured a guy called Charlie Pride. Jo Ann Castle and Joe Feeney told me I had to go hear this great singer, so I went along with them the last night we were there. They were right; he was really something.

After his show, I introduced myself and asked if he would be interested in making a guest appearance on the Welk TV Show. I told him that I couldn't promise anything. He gave me a recording he had just made and a photo. When I got back to L.A., I told Lawrence about Charlie Pride and gave him the recording. One thing Welk liked was music with a good beat. As soon as he heard the music playing, he started tapping his foot. That was a good sign. By the time Charlie's record was into the second chorus, Lawrence was clapping his hands and jumping up and down, so then I showed him Charlie's photo.

"Do you have his phone number?" Lawrence asked. "Maybe we can work something out."

He contacted Charlie and gave him a guest spot on the show. He sang "Lovesick Blues" and "Kaw-Liga." It was the first time Charlie had ever been on television, but he came off like a real pro. We invited him back a few times after that, and Lawrence wanted to hire him. But Charlie's manager wanted a contract and several other benefits. Welk didn't like to deal with anyone who had a manager. No one in the show ever had a contract. It was a handshake, with trust between him and the performers. But in this case, Charlie came out okay. Within the next couple of years, he became one of the biggest country singing stars in the business, and he's still going strong. It couldn't have happened to a nicer guy; I considered Charlie Pride a good friend.

Kathy Lennon once told me that I could sell the dirt on the stage. I took that as a compliment. You learn so much from performing over the years, and it's important to remember anything that gets a good reaction. Of course, there's a big difference between live stage and television. It was such an advantage to see myself on TV because it gave me an opportunity to observe and study the things I didn't like about my performance. That goes for ideas too. Mary Lou and I always did skit routines that told a story. When I watched them at home later, I liked some better than others. Staging ideas were so important. Mary Lou and I had similar thoughts about routines, so that made it much easier to work together.

Dancing with Art and Bobby was fun too. Sometimes we challenged each other in the middle of a routine, and that always got a good reaction. Lawrence liked that. Tap dancers, or hoofers, had what's called applause-getters, or "shine steps." If you did them right, they always got applause. Some of them were actually easy to do, but they looked difficult. One of the secrets was to make the audience think you were working real hard.

Jim Hobson was responsible for the look of our routines. The camera angles had to be favorable, and Rose Weiss' choice of costumes had to compliment what we were doing. It all added up to teamwork. On the day of the taping, we started at ten in the morning to rehearse each number on camera. We had a lunch break from one to two in the afternoon. After lunch, we continued until five. Dress rehearsal was from five to six o'clock, and we taped the show from eight to nine. We seldom had to interrupt a taping because of some technicality. It was amazing how Jim could pull it off so smoothly; he really held that show together. The most difficult time for all of us was when we had double taping of two different shows back-to-back in the same week. The performers always stepped up when this happened, and there were few hang-ups. All of the Welk Stars were true professionals, and that went for the crew as well.

Jim Baldwin was a talented cameraman on the show for many years and worked hard to make the Welk Show a success. He was later promoted to assistant director, also serving on the production staff. He had good ideas and was a big help to Jim Hobson.

Doug Smart was an up-and-coming director-type person who knew camera techniques and had valuable production ideas. Doug helped me with set-up on the road. He later became a professor and taught television techniques. He did a fantastic job directing a pilot TV show for Ava Barber and Dick Dale at their theater in Tennessee. Doug learned from Jim Hobson how to tape a show without going over the allowed budget.

Our art director, Chet Coons, could change a barn into a church overnight when we double-taped. Double-taping was a challenge to the singers too. When they had a solo on both days, plus at least three group numbers, that meant learning eight songs, not only the lyrics, but the moves I had given them as well. Sometimes I had trouble remembering the moves myself.

Some of the group numbers were prerecorded, but Lawrence wanted a lot of close-ups, so you had better know the lyrics. He watched every number from his dressing room on a monitor. Everyone received a cassette to help get the lip sync just right. The hardest day of the year was opening night at Harrah's in Tahoe. We rehearsed for two days, and the second day was a back-breaker. We started at ten in the morning, took an hour lunch, and finished the rehearsal around six o'clock. Then we performed two shows that same night. The first one started at 8:15 p.m. and the second one at midnight. It was a long day for Lawrence too, but with his lively energy, you would never have known he was tired.

After a rigorous opening night, we were then free every day after that. No more rehearsals, but we still performed two shows every night with no nights off. Lawrence and several of the cast members played golf almost every day. A few people had boats, and of course, there was always a casino ready to take your money. We all loved the three weeks we spent at Harrah's once a year.

We felt terrible when Bill Harrah passed away in 1978. He had treated us so well, and we always looked forward to that engagement. The Harrah family decided to sell their casinos to the Holiday Inn Corporation, but these new executives were not sold on the Welk Show. They wanted entertainers that would appeal more to the gamblers.

We always drew big crowds for every show, but only a few of them ever stayed around to gamble in the casino. In those days, having dinner and seeing a show was much cheaper than now. The casino made its money from the gamblers. We did our last engagement at Harrah's after having played there for seventeen years in a row. Welk really missed the association he'd had with them after such a long time.

I played the drums quite often with Myron Floren when he took the band out for special occasions. One time we played a convention in Vegas with Rudy Vallee. He passed out his charts to Myron, and we had a talk-through with Vallee just before his show. On one of the arrangements, the drum part had written on it in big letters "Play the *blank* out of it," *blank* meaning a four-letter word that starts with "S," and that's just what I did. After the show, Myron asked me why I had played so loud in one of the arrangements. I told him what was written on the chart, and I just assumed that it meant to play loud.

Musicians have always had to follow certain rules, especially in big cities like New York, Los Angeles, and Chicago. In New York, musicians were not allowed to walk through the lobby of a hotel. They had to use the alley entrance and go through the kitchen, which was extremely difficult for drummers. You had to find a bellman with a cart, and you better be a good tipper if you wanted help packing up after the job. You usually had to pass through the kitchen to get to the ballroom, which didn't make you very popular with the cooks and waiters. I always dreaded playing a certain hotel in Los Angeles, but piano players had it made because they used the house piano. The same rules applied to performers: you entered through the kitchen. Performers received better treatment from the hotel staff, however. If you impressed the hired help, you stood a better chance of getting a return engagement.

That went for the theaters too. I learned at a young age to be kind to the stage crew because they had a big influence as to whether you were invited back. I knew a lot of stars who went out of their way to be nice to the crew and musicians. When I set up the Welk Show on the road, I always tried to keep a pleasant attitude toward the people I worked with. Naturally, some stage crews were easier to deal with than others. Since the Welk Show often repeated many of the same venues, I always made notes to make it easier for me to remember when we came back to one that had been difficult. Being agreeable always paid off, and I usually got what I asked for.

One night Lawrence asked the crew if I had been easy to work with, and they told him everything was fine. I had to be careful to work both ends. If I had been demanding and difficult with certain crews, it might have gotten back to Welk. When you worked for Lawrence, you needed to have a good attitude with everyone. I learned so much from producing, and I know that being behind the scenes made me a better entertainer.

SIXTEEN

SUMMERS ON THE ROAD

I couldn't write this book without mentioning Bill Daly, a promoter for Welk during the fifties and sixties and several other big stars in the music business, including Duke Ellington and his orchestra. Bill was a captain in the Army and saw combat in the South Pacific. He lost his arm from a hand grenade that landed in his foxhole. Bill was successful promoting the Welk Show, but of course, that wasn't much of a gamble. Just one ad in the newspaper was all it took to sell out any arena in the country.

Bill booked the show at Keel Auditorium in St. Louis, which held over 10,000 people. It should have been a huge date, except for one oversight: It was the night of the Kennedy-Nixon election. Welk wanted to cancel, but Bill assured him that everyone would be tired of watching the returns on television, and he would have a big turnout at the gate. Well, it was a disaster. Only about three hundred tickets were sold. Can you imagine what that looked like in a place with 10,000 seats? Welk was furious. Bill lost thousands of dollars, plus Welk's reputation was at stake. The media didn't say much about the incident, but it meant the end for Bill as promoter of the Welk Show.

A couple of years later, Bill asked permission and got the okay from Welk to take a few of the performers on one-nighters with Myron Floren. It would be called *Myron Floren with Stars from The Lawrence Welk Show*. I helped with the production and did my act, and the show went on for several years. We worked about twelve dates a year, mostly in the springtime when it didn't interfere with the taping of the Welk shows.

We usually had a good turnout, but during one date in Little Rock, Arkansas, things didn't work out as planned. Bill was told that the audience was small, but it would pick up on the day of the show. Little Rock had a reputation for small advance sales, but big turnouts at the gate. On the day of the show, Bill and I took a cab to the venue. We were about four blocks from the theater when we ran into a huge traffic jam with people coming from all directions. We arrived at the stage entrance, and Bill was overjoyed to see the parking lot was packed. "It looks like a sellout," he said.

Bill Daly (left) had an easy time of it promoting the ever-popular Lawrence Welk, one-nighter road shows. They almost always attracted a sold-out crowd.

Once inside, Bill peeked through the curtain and was surprised to see only about a hundred people sitting in the audience. He went over to the stagehand and said, "I don't understand. The parking lot is full, and a lot of people are waiting to get in, but there's hardly anyone in here. Where is everybody?"

The stagehand looked at Bill and said, "Well, this theater has two sections, and in the other side there's a guy wrestling an alligator."

I thought Bill's mouth was going to drop clear to the floor. *The Myron Floren Show* had just been upstaged by a guy wrestling an alligator. To make matters worse, during the show when it was time for Joe Feeney to go on, we couldn't find him anywhere. Why? Because Joe was next door watching—you guessed it!

Poor Bill, it just wasn't his night. He was a kind and thoughtful person who managed to overcome his physical handicap. He was a good friend, and I took him with me on a cruise once. Afterward he told me it was one of the best times he ever had. Bill passed away from a heart attack and is missed by the Welk performers and everyone who knew him, especially me.

Frank Taylor, one of the best agents in Chicago, was a good friend of mine. He was married to the famous singer Wee Bonnie Baker, who had a big hit record with "Oh Johnny" in the late 1930s. He was also married to the Queen of Burlesque, Gypsy Rose Lee. Frank had been a tap dancer in vaudeville and understood what a hoofer goes through. He booked me on several fair dates in the Midwest. Another agent I worked with was Warren Bills, who used to be the drummer in the famous Ted Weems Orchestra. It was great working with agents like Frank and Warren because they had so many stories to tell about their experiences with show people.

My friend Dick Kerr had more talent than he knew what to do with. He was a comic and did great voice impressions of famous singers. We used to work together on *The Horace Heidt Show,* and I later hooked him up with Welk for a tour of one-nighters. He had terrific stage presence, and audiences gave him a standing ovation everywhere he performed. Dick made an appearance on the Welk TV show, but there was one problem. Dick needed more than two or three minutes to reach an audience, and our numbers were only three minutes long at the most. We had to squeeze twenty-two numbers plus five commercials into one hour. It was difficult for Dick to show what he could do in such a limited time. Later on he did a lot of entertaining on cruise ships. One thing for sure: I'm glad I never had to follow his act.

After our engagement at Harrah's every June, we usually went on a ten-day tour. This left July and August open for personal appearances, which were booked by Sam Lutz. Several of us kept busy every summer with bookings for fairs, home shows, or conventions. When I did fair dates, I performed for twenty or thirty minutes with all kinds of acts: trained animals, circus acts, and comedians. I always had a different band and only got to rehearse with them for a brief period of time.

First of all, it required four cases to pack up my marimba. They weighed a total of 125 pounds, and they had to fly with me. In those days, there were no security inspections of luggage, but you had to pay extra for excess baggage. It would be nearly impossible to travel like that today with all the airline restrictions. I had to worry about whether all the cases and luggage would make it onto the same airplane as me. If one case didn't make the flight, I was up the creek.

I always carried my musical arrangements onboard with me for safekeeping. After we landed, I had to rent a vehicle large enough to hold everything and then drive to the fairgrounds. Amazingly, I experienced only one close call, which was on a trip to Des Moines, Iowa. One of my cases didn't make it, and I still had to drive a hundred miles to get to the fairgrounds. The next flight into Des Moines wouldn't arrive until seven that evening, and the show started at eight—not much time.

There were four acts, and fortunately I was the closer, which gave me a little leeway. They sent a car to the airport to pick up my case, and I could only hope it would arrive in time. The show started right on schedule—but no case yet. At nine o'clock, still no case. Now the third act was on stage, and I was up next. They started to play the bow music for the act that I was to follow. I looked out across the racetrack and saw a man running with a case. It was mine! The emcee stalled while I scrambled to set up my marimba. I was a nervous wreck when that show was finally over. I couldn't tell you if my performance was good, bad, or ugly. The only thing I remember is that I did the show, and the check was in the mail.

One fair that I played provided only a piano accompaniment. It was almost showtime, and he hadn't arrived yet. The fair board told me he was going to be a little late, but not to worry, he could play anything. That usually means he's terrible—and he was. It was all I could do to force a smile; I felt more like crying. There was one part in my act where I tap danced without music. When I looked behind me to see if the piano player was ready to play the last part, I couldn't believe my eyes. He had fallen asleep at the keyboard! I might have been better off if he had slept through the entire act. When the show was over, I packed up my marimba, grabbed my check, jumped in the car, and took off, still wearing my tux and tap shoes.

I never knew what kind of band I was going to get. In some of the smaller towns, the musicians had second jobs because there wasn't enough work to make a living just being a musician. County fairs were one of the few opportunities for them to play. If the drummer had a picture of a lake painted on his bass drum with lights that go off and on, I knew I was in trouble.

The biggest problem was their inability to sight read. If they got a chance to play the music a few times beforehand, it helped them get familiar with the chart, but we never had much time to rehearse. Tempo was the most important thing for me. I didn't mind if they missed a note here and there, but the rhythm section had to keep the right beat. I never believed the saying: "The audience won't know the difference." If the beat isn't there, the audience knows something is wrong.

Of course, the sound system has to be right too. When you're downstage ten or twelve feet from the band, they have to be able to hear you. That would depend on how good the monitors are for the musicians. Playing an acoustical instrument in those days created a problem because marimbas didn't have amplifiers, so I just had to go with it. Weather could also cause problems. A sudden downpour could damage the keyboard and ruin the sheet music, so I always carried extra copies just in case. It was smart to come prepared because playing a fair was almost always an outdoor event. Some had tarps so the show could go on, even if it got stormy.

Some of the animal acts I worked with were really something. I'll never forget the flying mules. This guy had twelve mules that dove off a platform twenty-five feet high into a tank of water. They had to walk up a ramp, and the guy used a long stick with a spike on the end to jab them. When the animals reached the top, there was only one place to go—into the tank of water. The ramp was hidden from view, so the only thing the audience could see was a procession of mules falling off the platform into the tank.

During this act, the band played their theme song "Mule Train." When the mules heard that music, their ears shot straight up, and their eyes got big as banjos. They knew what that music meant: they were about to fall twenty-five feet into a tank of water. The man told me that he'd never had any kind of accident and no animal ever got hurt. I said, "Don't tell me, tell the mules."

Another animal act I shared a billing with involved boxing cats. The man had a small boxing ring with two holes drilled in the floor for the cats' tails. The man played the role of ringside announcer. The cats wore boxing gloves on their paws. He would pinch one cat's tail, and it would hit the other cat.

One time I was playing a fair in Skowhegan, Maine. I arrived the night before, so I decided to go over to the fairgrounds and check out the setup. I walked into the tent, which happened to be the men's dressing room. All of a sudden, I heard a roar that scared me half to death. I looked outside the tent and saw a lion in a cage with its trainer standing alongside. We introduced ourselves to each other, and he said he was the lion tamer for an act called "Bring 'Em Back Alive." His wife was also a lion tamer and the one who actually did the act.

He asked if I would like to see the cats, as he called them. We walked over behind the tent where he kept eight cages with a lion in each one. This was very interesting to me because I had never worked with or talked to a lion tamer before. During our conversation, I asked if he gave the lions a tranquilizer before the performance.

He looked at me with a straight face and said, "Oh, no, we would never do that because when the tranquilizer wears off, it makes them meaner. We have a much better method. We tap them on the head with a mallet. It makes them a little dizzy, but they are easier to work with."

"Which one of these lions is the meanest?" I asked.

"Oh, that would be Tonka."

We walked over to Tonka's cage. The bars were all bent and crooked. When Tonka saw us, he went out of his mind. There wasn't any doubt in my mind that Tonka took first prize. I was working with Joe Feeney at the time, so when I got back to the hotel, I told him that we had to see this act, and we caught the matinee.

"Bring 'Em Back Alive" had a portable cage that they set up for the act, and all the lion cages were placed in a straight line. The ends of the cages lifted up so it became a tunnel that led into the big enclosure where the man's wife was waiting with a whip and chair. The husband positioned himself at the end of the tunnel with his trusty mallet that he used to tap each lion as it came through. Tonka was the last lion to enter.

Mr. Mallet, as I called him, was waiting. Well, it wasn't a tap, or even a hit—it was a home run! Tonka made it into the big cage, but that was it. He sat on a riser and never moved. At the end of the act, Tonka walked slowly back through the tunnel. But I must say, the lady really knew how to handle the animals, and she got quite an ovation. I thought I had a lot to set up with the marimba, but it was nothing compared to the lion act.

I played the Arizona State Fair with a chimpanzee act once, and the man who trained them was very successful with these chimps. They traveled in an air-conditioned big rig and did a lot of movie work. He showed me some scars inflicted by his apes. He said they were strong and could be very dangerous after they reached a certain age. They were the opening act, and all the other performers were told to lock themselves in their dressing rooms. When the chimps came on stage, the password was "Chimps coming through." They were chained to each other, and when they passed each dressing room, they grabbed hold of the doorknob. It was a little scary hearing the chains and doorknobs rattling. The chimps didn't seem to realize they could rip those doors right off their hinges—and I wasn't about to tell them.

Fairs used to have what they called a special added attraction, either a circus or daredevil act of some kind. I worked with a man who would dive off a platform into a ten-foot tank of water. As the extra added attraction, he closed the show and asked me what my last number would be. I told him that when I started to tap dance, I was about ten minutes from the end. I didn't understand at the time why he wanted to know that, but I didn't think anymore about it. Well, it was because he had to set himself on fire on top of the platform. I had no idea he was going to perform this stunt immediately after I tap danced.

The audience was better than average that night, so I threw in a few extra steps, which made my dance longer than usual. Meanwhile, the man on the platform set himself on fire while I was still dancing. Imagine what the audience must have been thinking. Here I am dancing away, and a man on fire jumps sixty feet into a tank of water. Well, it sure put a finish to my act. From then on, if anyone asked me what my last number was, I told them to wait until they heard the bow music.

Probably the best daredevil act I ever worked with was for a home show at the old Cincinnati Gardens. "Captain Astronaut" was shot out of a canon at one end of the Gardens and landed in a net at the other end. The canon had to be set just right, or he would hit the top of the building. You only miss the net one time.

Captain Astronaut was the extra added attraction, and we shared the same dressing room during the eight days I performed there. When he was shot out of the canon, he would wave to the crowd right before he hit the net. Then he jumped up and took a dramatic bow. As soon as he was out of sight of the audience, he nearly collapsed. His wife would then help him back to the dressing room.

Every time I heard that canon go off, I knew he would be coming through that dressing room door about five minutes later, barely able to walk. That's what I call dedication. One night he looked at me and asked, "Do you know what I like about this date?"

"What?"

"There's no matinee."

He certainly earned every cent he made. I wondered how much he paid for life insurance. Irving Berlin's song, "There's No Business Like Show Business," really applied to Captain Astronaut. I've always had a great respect for circus-type acts.

They work hard for less money, and when they get older, most of them are forced to hang it up.

I worked for Ward Beam, one of the great booking agents, who created popular thrill shows. His professional drivers drove cars through fire and over ramps and did amazing stunts that the audiences loved. Ward was a stickler for how long an act should be on stage, and the fair boards were particular about how long the show ran in the amphitheater. They wanted the crowds to head for the midway after the show.

Fair boards received a big percentage of the money that the carnivals made. So when Ward said he wanted twelve and a half minutes, he meant it. He would sit in the front row with a stopwatch, and if an act was taking too much time, he would stand up and point to the wings, which meant your time was up. Thank God he never did that to me. Sometimes I thought he didn't care how good you were, only how long you took.

I worked a lot of fairs for Ward, and if I did what he said, we got along fine. Being on TV made me very aware of time. The reason performers got booked for so many fair dates was because of their exposure from television. I worked with performers who had been on television, and frankly, a few of them were a little disappointing. But it didn't make any difference; people just wanted to see in person the performers they knew from television. My being on *The Lawrence Welk Show* was certainly worth it for the exposure alone.

ABC carried a show called *You Asked for It* that was another version of *Ripley's Believe It or Not*. The show was taped, but they rehearsed the acts during the day of the show. One of the acts featured a man who called himself "Cannonball Jones." His specialty was catching a cannonball that was fired from a cannon twenty feet away. Well, during the rehearsal, the cannonball only went about ten feet. Cannonball Jones said there wasn't enough powder in the cannon, so they added more, and this time he caught the cannonball.

During the day, the stage manager decided they should put in more powder, just to make sure. A little later, Jones's manager did the same thing. Then right before the show, Cannonball Jones himself decided to add just a little more powder to the cannon. They taped the show at five. When it came time for

Cannonball Jones, they fired the cannon, and it flew clear over his head, through the wall, and into the next studio where they were broadcasting the news live. I guess there was a real panic on the set, but the news team kept on going. Cannonball Jones made history that night on the news, not only in L.A., but across the entire country.

SEVENTEEN

SEEING STARS

Being a part of *The Lawrence Welk Show* meant meeting a lot of celebrities and show business stars. Charlie Pride became a friend, as I said, but I also got to meet a lot of others such as Jack Benny, Pat Boone, Bob Hope, Johnny Cash, Barbara Mandrel, the Mills Brothers, Meredith Willson, Kate Smith, and Liberace. Lawrence always made a point of introducing me to them since I was the associate producer.

"I'd like for you to meet my bad boy," he always said to them. "Jack used to be a problem child, but then he became one of my most valuable people."

At Welk's suggestion, Bobby Burgess and I were going to work up a soft shoe with George Murphy when he came on the show. Murphy had done a lot of dancing in his early movies, so we got together and kicked around a couple of steps. But Murphy was in his sixties by then and decided it might be best to forget about it since he was running for a second term as senator of California at the time. He felt it might not be good for his image, and he should focus more on his campaign for office. So instead, he came up from the audience and said a few words on camera with Welk. He came across as a very likeable person.

I once did an autograph session with actress Virginia Mayo and she asked me, "Whatever happened to the music we used to listen to a few years ago?"

"Watch *The Lawrence Welk Show*," I answered.

I did another autograph session on a cruise ship with Glenn Ford. He complained that the flash bulb cameras were too bright.

I said, "Maybe they will invent a camera that doesn't need flash bulbs." Not long after that, they did.

Bandleader Ray Anthony stopped me on a cruise ship one day and said, "You must want to be the world's greatest marimba player."

"What do you mean?" I asked.

"A couple of my boys have the cabin next to yours, and they told me all you ever do is practice."

"Maybe it will rub off on them," I answered.

I performed at the Ohio State Fair with Henny Youngman and was sweating up a storm when I finished my act. He looked at me and asked, "What's the matter, kid? No confidence?"

The Welk Show was playing for a banquet at the Hollywood Palladium. It was a dinner and show affair that started at six o'clock. An hour before showtime, Lawrence wanted to lie down for about thirty minutes and asked me to wake him up at five-thirty. Several movie stars were in attendance that night. A little after five, I heard someone banging on the stage door—it was John Wayne.

"I want to say hello to Lawrence," he said. The Duke strode over to Lawrence's dressing room and started pounding on the door. "This is John Wayne, and I want to say hello."

"Mr. Welk is resting," I told him.

"Well, it's time for him to get up," he said.

Lawrence came to the door wearing just a robe. Wayne charged in and said, "I've been a fan of yours for years. I don't care what these people think. You're all right in my book." With that, Wayne left and returned to his table.

Lawrence looked at me and said, "Well, now I know what this audience thinks of me before we even start."

Needless to say, Lawrence put on a great show that night, and John Wayne led the crowd in a standing ovation at the end.

Afterward Lawrence asked me, "Isn't that the cowboy who plays in the movies?"

"He sure is."

I did a luncheon in Los Angeles with the famous second baseman for the Dodgers, Tommy Davis. After I finished my performance, I sat down beside him and lit a cigarette. "How can you dance like that and smoke?" he asked. After that conversation, I quit smoking for almost three years.

That same year, I presented an award to Gene Mauck, manager of the Philadelphia Phillies, at the Coliseum, and I got to sit in the dugout during the game. Some of the players were smoking in the back behind the bench, but Tommy Davis wasn't one of them. I told him I didn't smoke anymore and thanked him for encouraging me to quit. I'm not sure he remembered me, but he said, "That's nice."

I've made friends with several musicians through the years, including the talented Max Donaldson. We went to the Navy School of Music together and still see each other on occasion. Max and his lady friend, Linda Rae Roggensack, live in Denver and they helped me so much in editing this book. Besides being a drummer, he's also a writer, painter, and show business historian who travels all over the country giving talks on famous people. Max is a funny guy, always sending me jokes on a postcard. My mailman must think he's pretty funny too.

I'd also like to mention Clint Bookout, my good friend from Portland. We both worked at my dad's market when we were kids. We always go fishing together every time I go back home.

Another friend of mine is Ron McGehee of Redding, California. We first met at the Shasta County Fair in nearby Anderson, where he was the bandleader and tenor sax player who backed my act. We have been friends ever since. He's a pharmacist and still plays the sax on weekends at the Elks Club. Redding had a jazz festival and I played drums in his combo a few years back. Our families used to get together every year at Lake Shasta.

EIGHTEEN

ADIOS, AU REVOIR, AUFWIEDERSEHN

Whenever a TV show started to slip in the ratings, it always brought on a famous guest star to give it a boost, but this wasn't necessary with the Welk Show because celebrities were eager to come on to increase their own popularity. It kept a high and steady rating with syndication, and that reinforced a good relationship with our sponsor, J. B. Williams. But Father Time was starting to become a factor.

Lawrence was having trouble with his memory, and at times he looked a bit tired. When the 1981 season began, he was seventy-eight years old and still doing weekly television and at least ten one-nighters a year. Lawrence seldom came to the production meetings anymore and let Jim Hobson and George Cates make the necessary decisions. Lawrence always kept himself in top condition, and he certainly didn't have the appearance of a man his age. But everyone on the Welk Show believed their TV days were just about over and the show would soon be going off the air.

Jim Hobson came to me in January of 1982 with some discouraging news that Welk was seriously thinking about retiring. Jim said the Welk family wanted him to retire and enjoy the fruits of life that remained. It wasn't definite, but Jim thought this would be our final year. I agreed with him and kept our conversation quiet. I had heard rumors like that before, but with Jim, I knew it wasn't just a rumor. The production staff continued with work as usual, and I think we all gave Lawrence Welk one hundred percent. But that April it became final.

Jim Hobson met with the entire cast and explained the situation. We had four shows left to tape and a ten-day road trip in June. Our final show together would take place in Concord, California. The cast was very quiet, and a few tears were shed when Jim broke the news. At our final taping, the opening number was "There's No Business Like Show Business." I usually stayed out of the group numbers, but not this time, and I had a lump in my throat like everyone else.

After that taping, Jim showed us a two-hour video he had put together of numbers we had done throughout the years. We all enjoyed watching it, and none of us will ever forget it. All the wives and husbands were in the audience. Personally, I didn't know whether to laugh or cry when I saw the video. The Welk Show had been on television for twenty-seven seasons, and I'd been a part of it for twenty-five-and-a-half of those years. We had known it would all come to an end someday, but no one was really prepared for it. The only thing I had ever done during my entire career would now be taken away.

No one was old enough to retire, so we would have to find work elsewhere. But the worst part was that we wouldn't be working with each other anymore. We were truly a Musical Family. At least we still had a ten-day road trip to look forward to. We had always complained about going on the road—not enough sleep, traveling from town to town, nowhere to eat after the show—but now we were looking forward to this last road trip together.

One of the towns we played on that tour was Fort Wayne, Indiana, and it fell on my birthday. Lon Varnell, our promoter, met with the mayor's office, and the city decided to celebrate "Jack Imel Day" when we played there. Lon even paid for a plane ticket so that Norma could be there. Two busloads of people from Portland were given front-row seats for the show.

What a night it was for me. The mayor of Fort Wayne presented me with a plaque, and I got to see all my hometown friends. My best buddies Jay Miller, John Brigham, and Skip

Mallors went to Lawrence's dressing room, and he must have spent thirty minutes talking to them. That night Welk told the audience how valuable I had been over the years, and he repeated it three or four times during the show. There were more than 10,000 people in the audience, and it was one of the biggest highlights of my Welk years.

Longtime friend Jay Miller (center) met with Lawrence Welk and me backstage.

I was convinced that Lawrence thought I had done a good job. He had a profit-sharing retirement plan for everyone in the show, and several people like me, who had been with him all those years, received a healthy sum. What a wonderful way to end my twenty-five years with Lawrence Welk—and to think I almost turned it down for the Navy Band.

When we finished the tour in Concord, the audience was screaming, "Don't quit! Don't quit!" The girls were crying. Some of the cast members held out hope that Lawrence would return to television, but I didn't have any strong opinions about it either way.

Welk's television days weren't over yet, however. Syndication decided to take some of our reruns and re-tape Lawrence's intros at his resort in Escondido. It was good advertising for the resort, and we were still getting exposure from television. Then they decided to feature some of us each week doing the intros that Lawrence had done. This was the beginning of a long association with the Public Broadcasting Service. The intros were taped twice a year by the Oklahoma Network and sold to PBS, featuring one of the Welk Stars.

Lawrence Welk Jr. then took over for his father, signing contracts with PBS and the Oklahoma Network every two years. PBS has been broadcasting the show for more than thirty years now, so I can honestly say I was with the Welk organization for over fifty-five years. I've been with the show the longest, second only to Dick Dale. My job as a producer ended when we taped our last show, after which I focused on performing. After all, that's what I had been doing since I was twelve years old.

The Oklahoma Network did a tremendous job for the Welk Show. They taped all of the interviews with Mary Lou Metzger, as well as the hosting with Mary Lou and Bobby Burgess. In addition, they put together several specials that we taped at the Champagne Theatre in Branson. The Welk Show was renewed for two more seasons (2011-2012) on PBS for a total of fourteen years and counting. The Oklahoma Network had a wonderful staff, and they were great to work with:

Foundation president Bob Allen worked with Mary Lou on the pledge drives and had a lot to do with the production of our specials.

Station manager Bill Thrash directed most of the tapings. He's a very talented man and a fine jazz piano player.

Jo Ann Young wrote all the dialogue for the interviews, the hosting, and the quarterly Welk newsletter. She was also one of the producers for the specials.

Leon Smith, the main cameraman and light director, was in charge of editing.

Shirley Lee did a super job in charge of makeup.

Donna Spira inherited the rights to all of the Welk television shows from her husband Charlie, who passed away several years ago.

Mary Lou Metzger didn't have a title, but she played a key role in the success of the show on PBS and its pledging efforts.

Most important of all, of course, are the millions of fans who continue to watch our show each week. Many of them have been faithful viewers ever since the show first aired on television in 1955—over half a century ago. And let's not forget Larry Welk Jr. who did so much to keep the Welk Show popular since the last taping in 1982.

NINETEEN

OVER THE OCEAN BLUE

One day I received a call from Bing Crosby's brother Bob, who had a popular band for many years called the Bobcats. He needed a drummer who could also entertain. Bob was booked on a cruise ship for two weeks and wanted to know if I would be interested in joining his group. Well, of course I was interested. The cruise director was impressed with my work and asked if I could do a single, so they booked me for two months.

This was the start of almost ten years of performing on cruise lines—and I could take Norma along too. During that time, we got to see almost every corner of the world: the Caribbean, Panama Canal, Alaska, and the Orient, including Japan, China, Korea, and Singapore, and South America, clear down to Cape Horn.

Most of my bookings were handled by my agent Jackie Bright. The cruise ships did a lot for single acts such as comics, ventriloquists, dance teams, magicians, even jugglers (which was quite a feat on a moving ship), not to mention tap-dancing marimba players. Most of the time, I sailed with Cunard, Royal Caribbean, Crystal Harmony, and Holland America. It gave me the chance to work with a lot of famous people: Patty Andrews of the Andrews Sisters, Patti Page, Kay Starr, Jack Jones, Sid

Caesar, Jim Nabors, George Shearing, and even movie stars such as Glenn Ford, Jane Russell, and Virginia Mayo. It was a wonderful experience for both Norma and me, and sometimes my sons Greg, Tim, and Terry, or friends joined me.

Max Donaldson, my longtime buddy from the Navy School of Music, accompanied me on several cruises. Here we are going ashore to play some golf in Acapulco. Congratulations to Max, who recently aced a hole-in-one.

It wasn't easy playing the marimba—and especially tap dancing—when we ran into choppy waters. One night I was playing "Stardust" on the marimba when it started to roll off the stage. I had to stop and reset the instrument; Hoagy Carmichael probably turned over in his grave. The bands that backed me up were always good musicians, which made it pleasant. On a seven-day tour, I only had to perform two nights. They wanted two different 30-minute shows, so I needed an hour of material. It was a little hard at first, but after a few weeks I managed to work up a lot of new arrangements, so I had enough material and felt comfortable with it.

I had only one bad experience onboard a ship. I tore some ligaments in my left leg while dancing during rough seas and had to cut the act short. It was all I could do to finish the first show. I limped off the stage and told the crew director I couldn't perform the second show. He wasn't convinced and sent me to the ship doctor, who wasn't any help either. When we arrived in

Acapulco, the captain of the ship sent me to a doctor for an x-ray. Unfortunately, the x-ray didn't show any signs of a pulled ligament, and the captain accused me of faking it. He warned me that if I didn't perform, I would have to get off the ship.

Even though I could hardly walk, I was put off at the next port, along with my marimba. I was stranded, to say the least. I finally found transportation to the airport that could handle my marimba and was able to catch a flight back to Los Angeles. What made me so mad was how they refused to believe that anything was wrong with my leg. It was my first time working for that particular cruise line, and it was hard for me to accept that they thought I was a phony. I had never missed a performance before, and I felt terrible about it.

A couple of times, I did have a problem getting to the ship. Once when I flew to Santa Rosa, Costa Rica, I had to spend the night in a hotel and go aboard ship the next day. Holland America sent a driver in a station wagon to pick me up at the airport and take me to the hotel, which was about fifteen miles away. We loaded up and started for the hotel. About five miles from where I was staying, we noticed a fire in the distance.

"That fire looks like it might be close to the hotel you're staying at," the driver said. We drove a couple more miles. "That's really close to where you're staying."

Two blocks from the hotel he said, "I think your hotel is on fire." We pulled up in front of the burning building, and the driver got out of the car.

"I'll check you in," he said, while I stayed in the car. He came back out and said, "Well, you're all checked in."

"What do you mean I'm all checked in? This place is on fire."

The driver looked at me and said, "Only one side of the hotel is on fire. The part you're staying in is okay."

"That's what you think, amigo. I'm not staying at a hotel that's on fire. Take me to a different hotel."

"But I was told to bring you here."

"I don't care what they told you, I ain't staying here. This place is on fire."

The driver finally took me to another hotel. The next day I heard they did put out the fire, but I always wondered if that meant my room too.

Another time I flew to Rio de Janeiro to board a ship, and they picked me up at the airport. "We will have to go through Customs first," the driver said.

I was approached by the man in charge who asked what was in the cases. I explained that it was a marimba and I was going to a cruise ship.

"We'll have to take everything out of these cases," he said. I emptied them, and the agent came back later.

"You can put everything back in the cases," he said, without even looking at the different pieces. So far this had taken at least two hours. My driver got tired of waiting and left.

"It's going to cost you $500 to bring this into the country," the agent said.

When I told him I didn't have $500, he asked if I had any credit cards. When I said no, he told me to stay right there and he would be back. I saw him talking to another Customs man.

"You'll have to pay $250," he said when he returned.

By then I realized I was getting the runaround and told him that I didn't have $250. Actually I did have the money and credit cards too, but I wasn't about to let him know that. He left and talked to the same man again.

"How much do you have?" he asked when he came back.

"One hundred dollars."

"That will have to do."

I told him my driver had left, and I needed enough money to take a cab.

"The ship can pay the cab fare," he said, "and you'll need two cabs to handle all your equipment."

What a shakedown. When we finally arrived at the ship, I told them what had happened. The cruise line paid the cab and reimbursed me the $100 that I had given Customs. There was no doubt in my mind that things were a little corrupt there.

The most interesting places we visited were in the Orient, especially Shanghai, China. Over seven million people lived within a five-mile radius there. Bicycles and buses, plus a few taxis provided the only means of transportation. The people seemed very friendly. If you smiled at them, they smiled back.

China was a favorite port of call.

They loved having their picture taken, but they wanted to see the photo right then. We took a picture of a woman and her little boy, and they wanted to keep the picture. Her sister, who could speak English, explained that we didn't have a Polaroid camera. I said if she would give me her address, I would send her a copy after I got home. Norma and I did just that with a return address on the envelope. It never came back, so I can only assume they received it.

We found a department store called The Friendship Store that could convert our money into Chinese currency. They sold everything imaginable, and the prices were so much cheaper than at home. You could buy well-known brands of clothing, liquor, almost everything. Shanghai had very little crime, and it was truly a great experience.

Hong Kong was unbelievable too, but in a different way. It was more modern than Shanghai and had free enterprise. The people enjoyed a great deal more luxury and seemed to have a freer way of life. The Hong Kong skyline was spectacular. Tailor-made clothes were a great buy, sewn from materials of the highest quality. They took your measurements in the morning, and your clothes were ready by five that evening. Norma and I loved China.

Twenty

KEEP A SONG IN YOUR HEART

Lawrence Welk died in 1992 from pneumonia. We knew he had been having problems with his health, but it was more serious than we realized. He was eighty-nine years old, just ten years after his retirement. Almost everyone who had worked for him or was associated with him attended his funeral. Ralna sang his favorite hymn, "How Great Thou Art." When his body was carried from the church to the resting place, the band played his favorite kind of music, Dixieland. Alongside his grave, the Lennon Sisters sang "Adios," the song we always closed our TV show with. He was buried at Holy Cross Cemetery in Culver City, California, and the epitaph on his gravestone reads: "Keep a song in your heart." It was a sad day for all of us.

Lawrence had been responsible for so many wonderful things. He had given me and my family an abundant life and formed a foundation that helped me build for the future. His wife, Fern, along with his children Larry Jr., Donna, and Shirley, must have been very proud of all his accomplishments, not only as a showman, but as a husband and father as well. He received numerous awards during his long career, including a star on the Hollywood Walk of Fame.

After his father's death, Larry Welk Jr. took charge of the Welk Group organization, which oversees their resort interests, Welk Syndication, and the Welk Music Group. He built a very successful business selling luxury timeshares. Company interests include the Welk Resort in Branson and the Welk Resort and Champagne Village in Escondido, which features a restaurant, live Broadway musicals, water slides, spas, eight swimming pools, and two golf courses.

"Keep a Song in Your Heart"
March 11, 1903 to May 17, 1992

Twenty-One

BOUND FOR BRANSON

Larry Welk Jr. had big ideas for the future that involved the Welk performers. Branson, known as the "Live Music Show Capital of the World," was no secret to him. Nestled in the heart of the Ozark Mountains, Branson was already home to at least thirty theaters, some of them owned by major stars in the entertainment industry. Most of the venues featured country music, but there were other types as well.

Andy Williams had his own theater called Moon River. Then you had the Mickey Gilley Show, Jim Stafford, the Bobby Vinton Show, and the Osmond Brothers, just to name a few. But the biggest draw was the legendary Japanese violinist Shoji Tabuchi. He mostly did productions with young singers and dancers, and his signature number was "Orange Blossom Special."

Most of the audiences come to Branson on bus tours. The town offers many restaurants and attractions that appeal to the whole family. Winter, the most popular season for visitors, features a holiday celebration known as "Christmas in the Ozarks." The shows present mostly Christmas music with elaborate scenery and costumes. During the summer months, Table Rock Lake is a favorite destination. A huge showboat delivers entertainment like they had back in the 1800s, but it's been updated so it appeals to the audiences of today. You could spend weeks there and not see all the attractions this town has to offer.

Larry visited Branson and was impressed with what he saw, knowing that the Welk Show would fit right in with its family-type entertainment. He decided to build a theater that would be the only show in town with its very own hotel. It would, of course, be called The Champagne Theatre, starring the Lawrence Welk performers.

We were all pretty excited when we found out what Larry was doing because this brought us a lot of work. He booked the Lennon Sisters, Jo Ann Castle, and Ken Delo for the entire season from April through mid-December, and alternating a stable of other Welk stars throughout the season.

I always enjoyed performing with the talented Jo Ann Castle and Joe Feeney.

The producer and director of the show was Andre Tayir. He was familiar with some of the Welk people and had put together an act for Jo Ann and Tanya after they left the TV show. I worked a total of fifteen weeks that first year in 1994. We did two shows a day, with one day off each week. During the course of the year, we used a lot of performers such as Myron Floren, Bobby Burgess and Elaine Balden, Tom Netherton, Jim Roberts, Joe Feeney, Ralna English, Art Duncan, Mary Lou Metzger, Anacani, Dick Dale, Ava Barber, and Henry Cuesta.

When a busload of people from my hometown of Portland came to see our show, one man described their schedule to me. They saw nine shows and ate in nine restaurants in three days. He said by the last show each day, he was ready for bed. We could always tell when we were the final show on their schedule. Everyone was worn out from clapping, but they were a good audience.

After each show, we went out to the lobby and signed autographs for at least thirty minutes, which was something we enjoyed doing. These people had kept us on television all those many years. Norma and I loved Branson, and we made a lot of friends there. During the fourth season, Andre and Larry asked me to work the entire year, which I did for the next three years. Ava Barber was also hired for the entire season.

Norma and I rented a condo across the street from the theater in a gated neighborhood with a lake and golf course. Living in Branson was the most wonderful time of my life. I loved to fish and play golf, and everything was right there within walking distance from our home. The last year that I played the whole season, we had nearly a month off during the summer, so Norma and I were able to spend some time in Portland, which was about six hundred miles away.

Then one day, Andre decided to leave the show. Andre had already put the show together, but Larry needed someone who could deal with any problems that might come up. Larry asked if I would oversee everything at the theater. It would just be temporary until they found a new producer, so I agreed.

During this time, the Lennon Sisters asked for two days a week off instead of only one. Larry wanted me to come up with a show without the Lennons that would play just one day a week in their absence. I agreed, even though I hadn't produced a show since the TV days. It meant a lot of extra work for the cast, but I was able to put something together, and it worked out pretty well.

It takes a few weeks for a new show to start rolling, which complicated things a little. After a performance, it would be another six days before we did it again. Cast members sometimes forgot the staging, along with other things, and that included the stage crew and me as well. Trying to remember two different shows a week could be confusing, so it was a huge relief when they found a new producer and the Lennon Sisters came back fulltime.

The following year went fine, but the crowds seemed to be getting smaller. John Fredericks, Lawrence's grandson, was manager of the Welk Resort. He and Larry thought the show needed some new faces. He informed Ava, Jo Ann, and me that we wouldn't be working fulltime the next year. Maybe that change was for the best. After all, Welk had a lot of performers that our audience liked to see. Frankly, I wondered why I should be one of the chosen few who got to work the Champagne Theatre, so I went back to being one of the alternate acts. Our clarinetist, Henry Cuesta, replaced me.

The next season when I came back as an alternate, Henry asked me if I would play "Sing, Sing, Sing" with him on the drums. This was no ordinary number. It had been a big record in the 1940s that featured Gene Krupa. I hadn't played drums for years, but Henry said he thought I could do it with some practice. I was no Gene Krupa, but maybe I could at least do a decent job trying. I practiced hard for a month, and my technique started to improve. I was surprised by how well it went the first night, and it seemed to get even better as the nights rolled along.

I loved playing the drums and was glad Henry had talked me into it. Little did I know that I'd still be playing that number with him right up until he passed away in 2005. Henry was not only a great clarinet player, but a real showman as well. He suffered from throat problems, but he had so much heart that he kept right on playing until he died of cancer. We all miss him.

Joe Feeney is another one I miss. We were very close friends and had many good times together. Joe, Jo Ann Castle, and I went out on the town together more than once.

When Larry Welk built the Champagne Theatre, it was perfect for televising PBS specials. We had done several shows like that, and the most successful one was "Milestones and Memories," which featured almost everyone who had ever been on *The Lawrence Welk Show*. For that special, we brought in four of the Champagne Ladies who had been with Welk, dating back to the late 1940s. Bobby Burgess performed with all three of his former dance partners, Barbara Boylan, Cissy King, and Elaine Balden.

Bobby knew every ballroom step going back to the turn of the century, including the cakewalk, which had been popular on showboats. He could also tap with the best of them. Bobby started out on *Mickey Mouse Clubhouse* in the 1950s, and you had to have a lot of talent to be chosen by the Walt Disney Studios. I couldn't believe some of the lifts he did with his dance partners. He designed his own choreography and created some wonderful production numbers. After Bobby broke his foot doing the polka, he actually worked up routines wearing a cast. Amazing! He still dances with Elaine, and they do shows together around the country.

Art Duncan is unbelievable as well. He has received many awards from different dance associations and is still dancing up a storm. His footwork is as impressive now as it was fifty years ago. Working with Art and Bobby was a great pleasure for me. Reuniting with all the Welk Stars on the "Milestones and Memories" show was one of the most exciting highlights of my career. I hadn't seen Pete Fountain for years, so it was a joy to accompany him on drums when he played a Dixieland number. It was hard to imagine at our last taping in 1982 that we would all still be working together in 2001. PBS and the Oklahoma Network deserve all the credit for that.

Bobby Burgess, Art Duncan, and I are "Puttin' on the Ritz."

Branson presents awards for outstanding achievements in about twenty-five categories: best instrumentalist, best comic, best singer, best show, etc. In 1998 I received the award for best specialty instrumentalist. Hundreds of musicians and entertainers perform in Branson, so I was honored to have won this award.

Prior to Branson, many musicians had been working in Las Vegas, but in 1990, the Musicians' Union lost their court case against the big hotels and casinos. As a result, the restriction on using recorded music for big production shows was lifted, and live music became almost nonexistent. Many musicians lost their homes, gave up performing, and went back to teaching. A good number of them moved to Branson. I kept repeating how lucky I was to be working for Lawrence Welk, as many good musicians couldn't find steady work.

Twenty-Two

ONE-NIGHTERS

Meanwhile, Branson audiences for the Welk Stars were decreasing each year, so it was decided that we would perform only during the Christmas season from the first of November through late December. Larry Welk made Mary Lou Metzger the producer, and she did an excellent job in putting together some good group numbers and songs that everyone enjoyed. During this time, Larry introduced me to a Canadian promoter named Brian Edwards who wanted to create a Welk Show that would play in both Canada and the United States. Brian asked if I would be interested, and I answered with a big "Yes."

The following year, Brian took *The Live Lawrence Welk Show* on tour with seven Welk Stars and a ten-piece band to perform in the U.S. and Canada. We were seen regularly on television in Canada and were very popular there. We entertained big crowds in outstanding venues. When you worked with Brian Edwards, you went first class. We stayed at the best hotels and ate in the finest restaurants. Brian carried his own sound system, so there wasn't any guesswork. We would fly in to a major city and then bus it for four or five days at a time.

Frank Hewitt and John Lester were both outstanding in their jobs. I don't think I could've made it without Frank. He always saw that my luggage was with me and made sure I got my hotel key. They sold our merchandise such as CDs, cassettes, and programs. The program had everybody's picture in it, and we signed them for the audience after the show. Sometimes we had to leave right afterward and then sit on a bus for the next six hours—but that's show biz. We sure couldn't complain about that because we were still working and getting standing ovations.

All of our tours took place during February or March. You might say to yourself, Canada in February? Well, Canada is beautiful in the winter, and the people who live up there are prepared for any kind of bad weather. After our third tour, Brian made Roger Sullivan our stage manager, which was a good move because he always did a great job. The sound equipment traveled in a rig that was big enough to handle my marimba, so it stayed assembled. Through the years, that had always been my biggest headache, setting up and tearing down the marimba. Everything about Brian's tours was perfect for me.

Henry Cuesta joined the show and we did "Sing, Sing, Sing" together. He had already developed throat problems, but you would never have known it. He still sounded as good as ever. Mary Lou came up with an opening number called "Juke Box Saturday Night" that really got the show off to a rousing start.

Larry Welk also had the Welk Stars perform a Christmas show at the Welk Resort in Escondido, California. Mary Lou produced the show, and I did it several times. Tiny Little joined our group for Brian's one-nighters and was also on the Christmas show in Escondido.

I worked several shows in and around Los Angeles for an agent named Terry Hill. Some of the bookings included working with Horace Heidt Jr. and Les Brown and his Band of Renown.

Some of the Welk Stars performed at Bearcreek Farms, a 200-acre farm in rural Indiana that had been converted into a unique entertainment venue. The farmhouse became the Homestead Restaurant and the barn was converted into The Goodtimes Theatre that could seat about eight hundred people. It's located only ten miles from my hometown. They have shows year-round and are still going strong. I worked it five times and was able to draw quite a few people from Portland. Their band had excellent musicians from Indy and Muncie that backed the

Welk people. Norma always flew back with me when I played there, and one year our daughter Debbie came too.

Warren Bills, an agent in Chicago, did most of the bookings for the Welk Stars, including getting me into the Tulip Festival in Holland, Michigan, six times. He booked Myron Floren, Jo Ann Castle, Guy and Ralna, Mary Lou Metzger, and others all over the country. I can truly say that I've played every state in the union.

I used to have three marimbas, one in California and two that I kept with my friend Jay Miller in Portland, which I used for dates in the Midwest. I would fly to Indy, rent a car, drive to Portland, pack my marimba, and drive to the job. These dates were always spread apart with plenty of time to drive from one date to another. I didn't even attempt to fly the marimba during the last ten years. There were too many problems with security and excess baggage. Having three marimbas worked out fine, but more than once I wished I'd been a singer or a comic instead. That would have eliminated so many problems. But playing the marimba had opened the door for me, and I realized how important it was to keep playing it in my act since that's what I'd done on the Welk Show for so many years.

I continued to practice the marimba at least one hour a day, which was all I could handle without getting pains in my back. Sometimes I wore a brace, but that never seemed to work very well for me. You can't really improve with only one hour of practice a day, but at least I could keep up with the numbers in my act. I still tried to find time to practice tap dancing twenty or thirty minutes a day. But by then, I was in my seventies, so it wasn't getting any easier. People told me that tap dancing would keep me young. Well, that may hold true in some cases, but it didn't seem to work for me.

Norma's sister, Carolyn, had a recording of George Burns singing "Old Bones," and she kept saying how perfect it would be for me. I never thought of myself as a singer, so I didn't take her seriously. But finally I did listen to the song, and Carolyn was right—it was perfect for me, an entertainer in my seventies, thinking about retirement. The lyrics reflect on getting older, reminiscing about life's changes; they certainly echo my own sentiments. If I could turn back the hands of time and let my life begin, "Oh yeah, I'd like to do it again."

I took the song to Bob Smale, and he created an arrangement for me where I talked the lyrics, instead of singing them. I would sit on a stool, wearing a white straw skimmer. The first time I tried it out on stage, I received the most enthusiastic reaction I'd ever gotten for anything I had ever done before. "Old Bones" stayed in my act for more than ten years, and I even included it on my CD "Marimba Magic." It's funny how things work out. I have played the marimba and danced all my life, but singing "Old Bones" was so popular that I made it the closing number in my act. One thing about show biz, you're always learning, no matter how long you've been in the grind.

Twenty-Three

MEANWHILE, BACK HOME IN INDIANA

My hometown of Portland has changed and improved a lot since I left in 1952, although the population is still about the same. All the high schools were consolidated to form Jay County High School, ranking it among the largest in the state with more than 1,200 students and one of the best high school bands in all of Indiana.

The old Portland Armory became Jay Community Center with activities for adults and seniors and includes a Boys and Girls Club. Barry Hudson, one of the city's leading citizens, built a theater arts center. He has done so much for the community, including his latest project, a family park with a public swimming pool and an amphitheater for presenting entertainment. He's what I call a go-getter. I sold Barry some property that had belonged to my father, and now it's a housing development with a street down the middle called Jack Imel Avenue. It's only one block long and comes to a dead end, but I'm honored to have a street named after me.

The community center invited me to give a talk about my childhood in Portland and my experiences with Lawrence Welk. When I went back home for the event, a representative from the governor's office presented me with a humanitarian award called

Council of the Sagamores of the Wabash, one of the highest honors given to someone from Indiana. I'm really proud to have received such an award.

The Historical Society of Jay County makes a presentation every year to a citizen who has made a significant contribution to the county, and they invited me to come back for two days to accept this great honor. My family wanted to be with me for this special occasion, so fifteen of us flew to Portland from California for the celebration.

What a time we had. Five of my grandchildren, who had never been to my hometown, were among the group. They met cousins, aunts, uncles, and close friends of mine for the first time. They still talk about it to this day. It gave them a chance to see just how friendly people can be in a small town.

I didn't know that the Historical Society had a big surprise in store for me. They had highway signs made that proclaimed, "Portland, Indiana, Hometown of Jack Imel of the Lawrence Welk Show." The four signs were placed on both highways as you enter Portland. I was speechless. Nothing like that had ever happened to me before. I'd like to thank the Historical Society staff: President Kay Locker, Vice President Larry Bubp, Secretary Jane Spencer, Ralph May, Bill Gilpin, Ralph Grapner, and Jim Miller for making that tribute a moment I'll cherish always.

I was truly honored to receive an official proclamation from the governor's office announcing October 4, 2008 as Jack Imel Day.

I always enjoy getting together with my boyhood friends Clint Bookout and John Brigham whenever I go back home to Indiana.

My hometown of Portland, Indiana, surprised me by posting four welcome signs on the highways as you enter the city.

Mary Lou Metzger, Jay Miller, and Gail Farrell came to check out the marimba that I donated to the Historical Museum in Portland, Indiana.

The Jack Imel Day celebration in my hometown marked the end of my career as a tap-dancing marimba player at the age of seventy-six.

A street was named after me in the newly developed Imel Woods neighborhood of Portland.

TWENTY-FOUR

THE FAMILY TREE

GREG'S FAMILY

Our oldest son, Greg, attended Chatsworth High School in California where he played football. After graduation, he married Darlene Christian from San Francisco, and they had a son, Lawrence (Larry) Jennings Imel. However, the marriage had problems and resulted in a divorce. Greg ended up with custody of Larry, and they moved to Los Angeles to live with us. When Larry was six years old, Greg married Vicki, and they moved into a home of their own. This change was difficult for Norma because Larry had lived with us since he was an infant. A year later, Greg and Vicki had a son they named Gregory Shay. As teenagers, both Larry and Gregory played football at Westlake High School in Thousand Oaks. Norma and I attended all of their games, just as we had gone to the games of our sons when they were at Chatsworth High. Our son Greg is a hard worker and has been in the electronics industry since his twenties. Unfortunately, before the publication of this book, his wife Vicki passed away and will be missed very much by all of us.

After graduation from Westlake, our grandson Larry attended Pierce College for two years and then went on to UCLA where he graduated with a degree in political science. From there, he spent the next three years at Loyola Law School, graduating with a law degree. During his years in college, Larry lived with us; he's now a partner for a law firm in Beverly Hills. We are all very proud of Larry's accomplishments. He recently married Adriana, a girl from Romania. Larry's brother Gregory enlisted in the Coast Guard after he graduated from Westlake High. He's been in the service for twelve years and plans to make it a career. He has two children, Zachary and Anise.

DEBBIE'S FAMILY

Our second child, Debbie, also graduated from Chatsworth High School and married Kevin Gaspar. They had a son and a daughter, Timothy and Andrea, but their marriage ran into trouble and they divorced. Kevin and Debbie remain under good terms and are still friends.

Debbie is remarried to Ed Charton who has a son, Chad, from his previous marriage. Ed is a good family man and has been very successful in the insurance business and as a financial adviser. Debbie and Ed have two boys, Nicholas and Cory. Nick is six-foot-five and Cory is six-foot-eight, without a doubt, the tallest members in our family. Both boys graduated from Westlake High School; Nick goes to Moorpark Junior College, and Cory attends the University of California, Santa Barbara.

Our Grandson Timothy has always been full of ideas. After graduating from high school, he wanted to be in the music business, so he rented a small building in Canoga Park and turned it into a recording studio. He was financed by his father, Kevin, and stepfather, Ed, who purchased all the equipment for him. Tim found a singer that he thought had star potential, so they put together a demo and tried to sell it to record companies. It didn't take long for Tim to recognize all the problems that go into producing a hit, and he soon decided that it wasn't for him. Next he wanted to try his luck with a limousine service, but Kevin and Ed talked him out of that.

He then hit on the idea to make a water bottle with a compartment where people could hide their valuables, and he would sell them on eBay. Well, it caught on. People were buying them, but Tim made one mistake. He used the label from a major water company. When the company found out about it, they threatened to sue Tim for thousands of dollars unless he stopped the operation. Tim finally conceded and stopped selling the bottles. But he proved to his family that he was ambitious and wanted to make a success of himself. He went to college and graduated from the University of California, Northridge.

Tim now owns his own insurance company, and the family is proud of his accomplishments. He married Christina, a lawyer for the FBI, and they have a baby boy named Ryan Timothy. Tim and Christina recently attended a dinner in Los Angeles and had their picture taken with the President of the United States, Barak Obama. What a thrill that must have been.

Our granddaughter Andrea has really done well for herself. She graduated from the University of California, Santa Barbara with a degree in communications. She recently married Justin Pollock who is a financial adviser.

Debbie's husband, Ed, is really active. Along with his insurance company, he has a yacht, a Harley Davidson, and dune buggies. He's always taking his boys, Cory and Nicholas, someplace to ride their dirt bikes. Debbie owns Pearl's Knitting Parlor, a yarn shop that she named after my grandmother. Debbie has great taste in decorating her shop, just like her mother.

TIMOTHY'S FAMILY

Our third child, Timothy Jack, was a very bright lad, but college was not on his agenda. Instead he got a job working at a liquor store after high school and parlayed that into a liquor delivery service that encompassed all of Los Angeles County. Tim married Linda, and they had a son, Jennings Christopher Robert Anthony. Although the marriage broke up, they both devoted themselves to raising their son and making sure he had a college education.

Our youngest son, Terry, was working as a private investigator in the insurance industry when Tim expressed an interest in doing the same work. With Terry's help, Tim became a private investigator, and they worked together for the same company for six years until Terry relocated to Oregon.

Tim is now an in-house fraud specialist for a large insurance company. His fiancée, Sally Parry, is a sweetheart, and they've been together for fourteen years. She also deals with insurance fraud cases and has her own investigative firm. Tim was a member of the Chatsworth Neighborhood Council and has been responsible for several improvements in the community and at Chatsworth High School. One year he was named grand marshal for their homecoming football game. He loves to play golf and enjoys the hobby of constructing miniature Major League Baseball stadiums.

Our grandson Jennings Christopher Robert Anthony (everyone in the family calls him Chris) was an outstanding student. Not only that, he was an excellent musician, playing first chair trombone in a Southern California high school band; at age fourteen he performed in the Northridge University Philharmonic.

Chatsworth High has one of the best baseball programs in the country, and Chris played first base as well as pitcher for them. His senior year, they won the Los Angeles High School Championship and finished as national champions. Norma and I went to that final game, which was played at Dodger Stadium. Chatsworth High has also produced several major league players.

Chris was interested in politics and graduated from the University of California, Riverside with degrees in political science and Germanics. During the summer months while enrolled at UCR, Chris was an exchange student in Germany. After college he was a translator in the European Union. When he returned to the United States, Chris worked for a state assemblyman in Riverside County and became his campaign manager. He was accepted at George Washington University in Washington, DC, where he is working on a master's in foreign studies.

CINDY'S FAMILY

Our fourth child, Cynthia Diane, was married to Gary Buttner for several years before they divorced. They had two daughters, Jackie and Carly, and a son named Gary. Gary Sr. is a member of the Stagehand Union and works as a grip in motion pictures.

Cindy didn't like the idea of raising her children in Los Angeles because she considered it a bad environment. Jackie and

Gary Jr. were out of school by then and stayed with their father in the San Fernando Valley, so just Cindy and Carly moved to Porterville in the San Joaquin Valley.

Norma and I visited Cindy quite often, and she introduced us to Springville, about ten miles away and known as the Gateway to the Giant Sequoia National Monument. All the homes were custom built, with a golf course and a lake close by. It was perfect, so we sold our house in the San Fernando Valley and built a new home in the Montgomery Ranch area of Springville. The move made it possible to see a lot more of Cindy and Carly, but Cindy worked in Visalia, which was about forty miles from her home. It wasn't long before the daily commute became too difficult and inconvenient, so she and Carly moved to Visalia.

Carly became interested in dancing and enrolled in classes. She was good too! I started teaching her a tap routine that we could do together called "Me and My Shadow." She caught on pretty fast, but I could tell she didn't really take to that kind of dancing. She was more interested in hip-hop. However, she was creative and choreographed a routine that she performed in a dance school review.

After graduating from high school, Carly took a course in choreography at College of the Sequoias in Visalia. Later she went back to the Los Angeles area to live with her Aunt Debbie and Uncle Ed. She studied for a year at Moorpark City College, but then lost interest. It's kind of hard to keep up with the younger generation these days, but I'm sure she'll find what she wants to do with her life and will be just fine.

Cindy's son, Gary, moved to Fresno where he's a student at the Fresno School of Technology, learning to be a professional chef. He loves to cook, and he's terrific at it. Gary is smart and will do well in life. Her daughter Jackie stayed in the Los Angeles area and we see her quite often when we visit our family in the San Fernando Valley.

We see Cindy almost every week. Norma belongs to a Bible study group in Visalia and always visits her afterward. We try to make it down to the San Fernando Valley at least once a month to see our kids and grandchildren.

TERRY'S FAMILY

Our youngest child, Terrence (Terry) Mark, was outgoing and loved talking to people. He always had a job and saved his money. He took a couple of trips back to Indiana on his own right after high school. One year he told us, "I'll be home for Christmas, but I have a flight to Indiana for New Year's." I think it was after that trip that he decided to go to Ball State University in Muncie. Since his grandparents lived in Portland, just thirty miles away, he probably figured we would be okay with that. He tried out for the football team in the spring of 1978 and made the practice squad, but he quit when he realized he would probably never play.

Terry played semi-pro with the Anderson Packers football team, but it only took one winter for him to realize he had made the wrong choice. He came back to California with the idea of going to Pierce College in the San Fernando Valley. Just before his enrollment, he was offered a job coaching football at Faith Baptist High, a private school where you didn't need college credentials. He coached there for a year until he was offered a job with a private detective company handling insurance fraud. He worked as a surveillance investigator for the rest of his life. What an interesting job that was. He had a lot of stories to tell about people trying to scam money from insurance companies with false claims. He was innovative and had a talent for acting that helped him catch the people he was conducting surveillance on.

In 1987 Norma and I were shocked when Terry had a heart attack. I remember thinking this couldn't be true; he was too young—only twenty-seven—and healthy looking. He seemed to recover and decided to start his own business called Imel Investigations in 1989. Life went on. His business was doing well, but his health was always on my mind. In his spare time, he was into competitive bike riding. In 1992 he rode the fifty-mile Rosarito Beach to Ensenada bike ride in less than three and a half hours.

The following spring, Terry suffered a second major heart attack and had open-heart surgery. He lost everything because he couldn't be there to run his business. When he was released from the hospital, we took him to our house and put all of his belongings in storage. Reluctantly, he and his two dogs moved in with us. I know that's not what he wanted because he had always been so independent. It really bothered him not knowing what he was going to do next.

After about six months with us, Terry felt strong enough to apply for a job at HMI Investigation Company. To his surprise they hired him, and he moved into a condo. At that time, his brother Tim was looking for a new job, and Terry talked him into working at HMI also. Working together brought the two brothers even closer. In the summer of 1993, Terry met Paula, the girl he described as the love of his life. She had been married before and had a son named Seth.

Terry and Paula were so happy on their wedding day.

Northridge, California, experienced a serious earthquake in January of 1994 in the middle of the night. The epicenter was only ten miles from our home. We ran outside because we could hear a lot of cracking noises, and I thought the house was coming down. As we sat in the darkness in front of our house, the first person to show up was Terry. He thought he smelled gas in the garage, so he broke down the door and turned off the gas. When daylight came, we saw the fireplace in the living room had half fallen down, and an outside wall had collapsed into the backyard. The quake caused extensive damage, and we had to move out for over a year while the insurance company rebuilt our home.

Terry and Paula were married that spring. In August they had a son they named Forrest Clayton. Terry was so happy; everything he wanted in life was starting to come true.

Norma and I went to Branson where the Welk Stars were performing in the Champagne Theatre. Terry and Paula moved to Kaiser, Oregon, where her father lived, to raise their family. They bought a new home, and Terry reopened his investigative business. He was very lucky and started getting clients right away. At night he worked as a bartender in a bar that Paula's father owned. Everything seemed to be going well for all of us, but we were probably in denial about Terry's condition and what could possibly happen. On July 21, 1998, it did happen—he was only thirty-eight years old.

Norma and I had gone to bed early because our grandson Larry was coming to visit us. He had never been to Branson before, and we looked forward to showing him around. We were to pick him up at the airport the next morning at eight. Norma woke up during the night and said she couldn't sleep because she was so excited about Larry's visit. At 2:30 a.m. the telephone rang, and Norma answered it. It was our daughter Debbie.

"Is Dad there with you?" she asked. I knew immediately something was very wrong.

"Of course he's here," Norma answered.

"Terry is gone."

Norma and I went to pieces at this devastating news. Tim was there with his sister, and they waited on the phone as we broke down, sobbing. They say they will never forget the heartbreaking sound of our grief. I can't remember much more, except that Norma said she had to walk and ran out the door as I chased after her. We went down to the lake and sat on a picnic table, both of us crying. Lightning and thunder threatened nearby, and I remember telling Norma that we'd better go back inside because we were underneath a big tree.

The sorrowful night seemed endless. In a daze, we prepared to leave for the airport to meet our grandson and give him the terrible news. Before we left, Norma called our friend Marilyn Delo to tell her what had happened. She offered to pick up Larry for us, but we said no, we needed to do that ourselves. When we returned to our apartment, Jo Ann Castle, who had known Terry since he was a baby, was waiting at our door. She had lost a daughter and knew how we felt.

Norma had a travel agent friend in Los Angeles, and it took her two days to finally book us on a flight to Oregon. Young Larry helped us pack, and we all flew together. We drove a rental car to the hotel where our children were waiting. This is not a pleasant memory, but one that should be told. Every life tragedy can teach us something. Of this I am sure—God places us where He wants us to be. We were to be in Branson, and Larry was meant to be there with us. We were blessed to have the love and support of so many dear friends who understood our grief: Joe Feeney, Jim Roberts, Henry Cuesta, Jo Ann Castle, and Peggy Lennon had all lost a child.

I didn't ask "Why me, Lord?" I knew that someday we would come to understand why. In 2001 our son Tim obtained a private investigation license and named his firm Imel & Imel Investigations in memory of his brother.

Terry would be proud of his son, Forrest. He's a very good student with a talent for drawing. He hopes to become a commercial artist after college, and some companies are already interested in his work. He stays with us every summer, and his uncles, aunts, and cousins look forward to having a good time when he's here. His half-brother, Seth, is studying for a degree in music as a percussionist. I'm proud of all my grandchildren, and I know they will be successful with whatever they choose.

OUR PARENTS

I lost my father back in 1971, and my mother died two years later. That was a difficult time for everyone. Mom and Dad had done so much for me, and a day never goes by that I don't think of them. I can still see my dad carrying that marimba up and down stairways and loading it in and out of the car when I was working for Dorothy Durbin. Trying to raise my children the way I was raised proved very hard for me, even though they turned out fine. I still feel like I should have done more to encourage and help them. Norma deserves most of the credit for raising our family.

Lawrence Welk posed for a photo with my proud parents, Opel and Jennings Imel.

The hardest part about living in California was being so far removed from home and parents. I always found a way to take my family back to Portland, and my parents were able to visit us once in a while. But they didn't come just to see me, they missed their grandchildren. To this day, my children remember every time we went back to Indiana.

Norma's parents and older brother Dick have also passed away, so she has gone through the same sorrows. We miss our son Terry more than words can say. Children are supposed to outlive their parents. Thank the Lord we are able to see Terry's son, Forrest, from time to time.

Twenty-Five

THE GOLDEN YEARS

My so-called golden years started to lose some of the glitter, however, and life was becoming a bore. I had been able to control my drinking through the years, but now I found myself taking a drink a little earlier each day. In fact, I was helping myself to a Bloody Mary most of the day and into the evening. Norma was concerned and told me to slow down. Before long, I was hiding bottles around the house, even under the bed. It was getting out of hand, and I knew something had to change. It wasn't fair to Norma—after all, these were her golden years too. Finally she put her foot down and insisted that I get help.

I didn't consider myself an alcoholic, of course, but that is the first sure sign of having a problem. I reluctantly checked into a rehab center in Los Angeles, and those were the three worst days of my life. The place was filled with people of all ages, from every walk of life, not only alcoholics, but drug addicts too. According to the doctors, some of the patients return time and again for three or more weeks. When Norma and our son Tim visited me on the second day, I announced that I was cured, but Norma wanted me to stay for at least a week. It was hard to convince her and the doctors that I needed only three days, and I would never be back.

Norma and Debbie took me home the following day. I was nervous at first, but I kept thinking about those people back at the center and how miserable I felt there. Norma was still not convinced that I was cured, so I agreed to see an analyst for a couple of months. I'm happy to say that I haven't taken a drink for over five years now, and I don't have the least desire for one. Contrary to what the doctors had told me, that most clients come back three or four times before they're cured, I was one of the fortunate few who didn't need to. That rehab center changed my desire to drink, and I recommend it to anyone who has the same problem. I really feel sorry for all those who can't break their alcohol and drug habits. My family is proud of the fact that I no longer need a drink to get through the day, and I thank God for helping me overcome my disease.

I started to give some thought about retiring from the business I'd loved my whole life—I was seventy-six years old, after all! I didn't feel that my performance was what it should be anymore. There comes a day (hopefully) when a person just knows that it's time to get off the stage. Norma, Debbie, and I flew to Indiana for my last performance on June 3, 2008. Bearcreek Farms in Bryant, being so close to my hometown, seemed like the perfect place to end my career. I did a matinee and an evening show, and afterward they threw a party to celebrate my retirement. No more practicing and traveling from place to place. I knew I would miss everything that goes with it, especially the audiences. But at least I could watch the Lawrence Welk reruns on PBS and feel like I was still part of the business. After Bearcreek Farms, we flew back to California, and I started a new lifestyle.

Now that I was officially retired, I found myself with a lot of free time; some days I never even went outside. Norma, on the other hand, has a lot of energy and always manages to keep busy. We live on one-and-a-quarter acres in the countryside near the foothills of the Sierra Nevada Mountains. My children and grandchildren all live within driving distance of our home in Springville. We attend a Methodist church in Porterville that is only ten miles away and stay active with church events. Our neighbors are pleasant, down-to-earth people, and we've made friends with many of them. I've even been able to turn some of them into Lawrence Welk fans, who are now watching the show on Saturday nights.

One day I received a phone call from Brian Edwards, the promoter. "I know you don't perform anymore, but I'd love to have you do a tour with some of the Welk Stars in Canada," he said. "Could you put something together without the marimba?"

I told him I would think it over and let him know in a few days. My act had been built around the marimba, and I had never performed without it. What would I do? Maybe I could work out a number with Mary Lou. "Everything Old Is New Again" would be perfect. We could sing the first chorus sitting on stools and finish with a couple of dance steps. I could play the Glenn Miller arrangement of "St. Louis Blues" on the drums and close with "Old Bones." I wouldn't have to set up my marimba every night. It really sounded good to me.

I called Brian and said I would do it, but I wanted to take Norma with me. He said that was fine. Norma was really excited when I told her she was going on a two-week tour in Canada. I set up my drums in the garage and started practicing. Mary Lou and I worked up a routine, and I could hardly wait to start the tour. We opened in the Wisconsin Dells where we rehearsed for two days. Mary Lou put the show together with some great musicians we had worked with in Branson. The show included Dick Dale, Ava Barber, Gail Farrell, Mary Lou, and accordionist Jim Padilla. In early February, we all flew to Madison and took a bus to the Dells. From there we traveled by bus into Canada and enjoyed the beautiful scenery. Snow was on the ground, but the roads were clear.

I was really nervous that first night in Wisconsin, performing without the marimba. The Welk Stars never sounded better, and the audience loved it. Dick Dale was eighty-four years old, but he looked and sounded wonderful. Ava Barber could really sing a country song and had a lot of charisma. Gail Farrell played piano and had a great voice. Jim Padilla was a real showman on the accordion. Yeah, I know everybody sounded great—but that's the best way to describe it. Ava's husband, Roger Sullivan, was stage manager, and here again did a masterful job every night. We had all of the right ingredients needed to put on a show and got standing ovations after every performance. It certainly felt good being on stage again. Norma and I had a wonderful time being with the Welk people, as she's good friends with all of them. Maybe Brian will set up another tour in the future.

After the tour, Norma and I flew home to Springville, which is only three hours north of Los Angeles. We have so much to be grateful for, and we thank God for all our blessings. I almost forgot to tell you, we have two dogs: a dachshund named Alvin, who is thirteen years old, and a dachshund mix we call Kandi, who's only two years old. They usually stay with Debbie or Cindy when we take a trip. It's amazing how much we miss them when they're not with us.

Norma and I are enjoying our golden years together at our home in Springville, California.

Buck Schafer, director of the Porterville High School Band, was a faithful fan of the Welk Show and asked if I would be interested in helping him select talent for the City of Hope Show. Buck taught music and had spent most of his life trying to develop young talent. I accepted the offer and became a member of his committee. We auditioned more than a hundred kids who sang, danced, and played instruments. Some of them attended dance schools and performed in a group. It amounted to about twenty acts, and we hardly ever turned anyone down. Those dance groups meant lots of ticket sales to relatives and friends. They cost five dollars each, and we filled the high school auditorium every year. The City of Hope worked for a good cause in the fight to cure cancer.

Some of the kids showed potential, and we encouraged them to stick with their talents. Buck's son, Skip, was great on drums and even performed several times with Henry Cuesta. Buck has since died, and Porterville named the auditorium in his honor.

A word of advice to those who are thinking of retiring: keep busy. One way is to become active in your community as a volunteer. My work with City of Hope involved only two months of the year, so when my neighbor Linn Wiseman told me about the Lions Club, I was interested. He invited me to a meeting in Springville, which I enjoyed, so after attending three meetings, I was accepted as a member. It's well-known that the Lions Club does a lot to help the community by raising money for scholarships, city improvements, Boy Scouts, parks, all kinds of things. I've been a member for several years now and have missed only a few meetings. Many of their achievements require a great deal of work and planning. We have a lot of fun when we get together, but we're very serious about our projects. I'm proud to say I'm a Lion.

Twenty-Six

OH YES, I'D LIKE TO DO IT AGAIN

I recently celebrated my eightieth birthday. Where did all the years go! Is there such a thing as working hard, but still having fun? Well, that's the way it seemed to me. The marimba did not come natural to me. I had to practice at least two or three hours a day just to be average, but I never got to the point where I wanted to give it up. Now the drums were something else. I enjoyed the rhythm and loved to play the band charts. When I used to listen to recordings as a kid, I paid special attention to the drummer. There were so many good drummers back in those days.

The dancing came easy to me, except I didn't like the ballet part, even though it's important to every kind of dancing. It teaches you so much about control and building your body. Fred Astaire and Gene Kelly were excellent examples. When they danced, you could tell they had studied ballet. Tap dancing is difficult and demands hours of practice, but I did enjoy it. At least my footwork was good and clean. I learned early in life that it's not what you do, but the way that you do it.

Looking back on a lifetime in show business, I can see that Norma and I have some fabulous—or as Lawrence would say, "wunnerful"—memories. We met so many fun and fascinating people along the way.

I like to believe that most people take pleasure in their chosen profession, but show business is in a league all its own. It's kind of like sports. People applaud and show their appreciation when you do something they enjoy. That's what I miss most, now that I'm retired.

When I watch the Welk reruns, I think about all the good times I had with those talented people. Forty-seven members of the Welk Family have passed on since I joined in 1957, but thirty-nine are still going strong. We just signed with PBS for two more years, marking the thirteenth and fourteenth seasons for the Welk Show on public television. I extend my deep thanks to all the fans that supported the show throughout the decades. Like the song says, "If I had just half a chance to turn back the hands and let my life begin, oh yes, I'd like to do it again."

Oh yes, I'd like to do it again!

Additional copies of

Jack Imel: My Years with Lawrence Welk as a Tap-Dancing Marimba Player

may be purchased at:

www.JackImel.com

Made in the USA
San Bernardino, CA
29 March 2016